JARCUTERIE

JARCUTERIE

ELEVATE YOUR APPETIZERS AND
SNACKS WITH GRAZING CUPS
FOR HOLIDAYS, SPECIAL OCCASIONS,
AND JUST FOR FUN

SUZANNE BILLINGS

ROCK
POINT

Inspiring | Educating | Creating | Entertaining

Brimming with creative inspiration, how-to projects, and useful information to enrich your everyday life, quarto.com is a favorite destination for those pursuing their interests and passions.

Text © 2022 by Suzanne Billings
Photography © 2022 by Quarto Publishing Group USA Inc.

First published in 2022 by Rock Point, an imprint of The Quarto Group,
142 West 36th Street, 4th Floor, New York, NY 10018, USA
T (212) 779-4972 F (212) 779-6058 www.Quarto.com

Rock Point titles are also available at discount for retail, wholesale, promotional and bulk purchase. For details, contact the Special Sales Manager by email at specialsales@quarto.com or by mail at The Quarto Group, Attn: Special Sales Manager, 100 Cummings Center Suite, 265D, Beverly, MA 01915, USA.

10 9 8 7 6 5 4 3 2 1

ISBN: 978-1-63106-840-9

Library of Congress Control Number: 2021949233

Publisher: Rage Kindelsperger
Creative Director: Laura Drew
Managing Editor: Cara Donaldson
Senior Editor: Erin Canning
Cover and Interior Design: Laura Klynstra
Photography: Chelsea Chorpenning
Food Styling: Gina Nistico
With special thanks to Marissa Hagy

Printed in China

To my family, who has
lovingly and patiently
supported me in
everything I've ever
done. I love you, and I'm
so thankful for you.

CONTENTS

Introduction 8

The Benefits of
Jarcuterie 9

Tools of the Trade 10

The Graze Anatomy of
Jarcuterie 12

Getting Started 14

Food-Styling
Techniques 16

CLASSICS

Classic Jarcuterie 21

Mini Jarcuterie 23

Grazing Cones 25

Personal Charcuterie
Boards 33

Melon Caprese Mini
Boats 35

Charcuterie Kebabs 37

Edible Board Crostini 39

Tidbit Wine Toppers 41

Sidecar Charcuterie
Cones 45

Crudités Dip Cups 47

HOLIDAYS

Valentine's Day Chocolate
Cups 51

Saint Patrick's Day
Lucky Jars 53

Easter Egg Treat
Cartons 55

Mother's Day Teacups 57

Father's Day Grazing
Cups 59

Fourth of July Fireworks
Cups 61

Fourth of July Sparkler
Cones 63

Halloween Spooky Snack
Cauldrons 65

Christmas Charcuterie
Cups 67

Mini Christmas Tree
Boards 69

New Year's Eve
Coupe Glasses 71

SPECIAL OCCASIONS

Birthday Party Candy Jarcuterie 75

Movie Night Popcorn Boxes 77

Happy Hour Snack Mugs 79

Game Day Appetizer Cups 81

Home Run Snack Baskets 83

French Toast Breakfast Cups 85

Bagels and Lox Brunch Cups 87

AROUND THE WORLD & SEASONAL

Fiesta Jarcuterie 91

Greek Loaded Hummus Ramekins 93

Italian Jarcuterie 94

Asian-Inspired Appetizer Cups 97

Spring Flowerpots 99

Summer Clip-On Snack Cones 101

Sweet & Salty Fall Snack Jars 103

Winter Hot Chocolate Cups 105

JUST FOR FUN

Rainbow Boxes 109

Barkuterie Pup Cups 111

S'mores Kits 113

Farmers Market Gift Baskets 115

Snackle Box 117

Pencil Snack Box 119

Picnic Sandwich Packs 121

Recipes 123

Resources 135

Index 136

Acknowledgments 142

About the Author 144

INTRODUCTION

I've been at this grazing game a while. I love to entertain, and I'm always searching for unique ways to bring people together. Food is my favorite way to do that, and grazing is always a crowd-pleaser. When I started entertaining with grazing boards, my friends and family were always wowed by the presentation. It was a feast for the eyes, and they loved the idea of getting to sample a little bit of everything.

When the pandemic hit and social distancing became the standard, we were all yearning for connection and still wanting to entertain. Friends gathered at safe distances in driveways and yards, and I was seeing that most people struggled to find a safe and fun way to serve food. Large charcuterie and grazing boards and buffet-style presentations were discouraged. It was difficult to know the right way to entertain. I had seen food cones for years, but I wanted a more distinctive presentation. I brainstormed different options and settled on mason jars. Serving food in mason jars wasn't unique, especially in the South, but the way I put it together was. My intention was to translate a grazing board into a single serving, so everyone still got a taste of everything without having to share, in a form that was easy to eat.

I posted my first version of this idea on Instagram, and the response was overwhelming. Right away, I knew I was onto something that would be sticking around beyond the pandemic. I didn't know quite what to call it yet, but the idea was out there and taking off. My friend Emily, who is a great wordsmith, dubbed it "jarcuterie." Everyone loved the "charcuterie" play on words, and so did I! Now I'm happy to share my innovation with you through this book, and give you a reason to entertain.

What's my best advice for at-home entertaining? Just do it. Don't wait for an occasion. Don't wait for your house to be clean. Don't wait until you have the perfect table, chairs, dishes, whatever. Start bringing friends and family together sooner rather than later. You won't regret having friends and family over when your home isn't perfectly clean, but you will regret not having them over at all. Hide your laundry or stack up the bills and homework to clear the table if you're worried that anyone will care. People know you live in your home and that it's not just staged for a magazine photo shoot. Or move the party outside if weather permits and you're worried about a mess inside. Don't have the perfect outdoor furniture setup? Tell your guests it's BYOC (bring your own chair), or throw a few blankets and pillows on the ground. Anything goes, and individual servings will help make it fun and easy to clean up.

Single-serve options are here to stay—they're fun, visually appealing, and have all the taste and sophistication of a grazing board, but you don't have to share! Let your creativity guide you. Don't worry about precise recipes and doing things perfectly. Lots of components can easily be substituted according to your preference or what you have on hand. Take these ideas and make them your own.

I love thinking beyond the board, and you will too!

THE BENEFITS OF JARCUTERIE

Through my experience of creating and serving jarcuterie at so many different events, I have discovered many benefits that make this an ideal way to entertain friends and family.

NO SHARING

This is a big one for most people these days, and understandably so. Jarcuterie's individual servings help keep food safer and less exposed. Also, I don't know about you, but I don't want to share my food anyway. I love having a single serving all to myself!

CUSTOMIZABLE FOR DIETARY PREFERENCES

If you're having a crowd with mixed dietary preferences, you can easily customize jarcuterie by eliminating or adding ingredients. For example, you can easily make any option gluten-free by just swapping out crackers or pretzels. Also, vegetarians and vegans will appreciate having their own serving not touching any meat.

CUSTOMIZABLE FOR ANY OCCASION

Jarcuterie loves a theme! You can easily customize your single-serve options with a color scheme, decorative picks and flags, festive containers, specialty food items, or food cut into shapes with cookie cutters.

QUICK AND EASY SERVICE

It's much quicker to serve jarcuterie than a large grazing table or buffet. Guests can quickly get their serving and start mingling, or you can set their jarcuterie at their place setting. There's no waiting in a buffet-style line, no waiting on people trying to decide what to put on their plate, and no waiting on those who get distracted talking. Just grab and go! Plus, there's no hovering around the food, which helps to keep things more sanitary.

VISUALLY APPEALING

I can't tell you how much I love seeing guests' eyes light up or hearing them squeal with excitement when they see a display of individual servings ready to enjoy. It is unexpected, delightful, and even whimsical. You can easily take the visual appeal to the next level because there are so many beautiful containers to choose from!

EASY CLEANUP

This is definitely a favorite benefit of individual servings. A big burden of hosting is the cleanup required at the end of the gathering, but with jarcuterie, this is not an issue. You can either use dishwasher-safe containers or eco-friendly disposable containers, which means that there's not a lot of bulky serving pieces or boards to clean up.

TOOLS OF THE TRADE

Having the right tools on hand for prepping and assembling ingredients for jarcuterie will make the process go smoother and faster. Here's what I recommend, and what I personally use, to make things easier.

CONTAINERS

You can't have jarcuterie without containers! If single-serve options are going to be your go-to for entertaining, I suggest keeping an assortment of containers on hand, from reusable (and dishwasher safe) to disposable. They should range in size from 4 ounces (120 ml) to 9 ounces (270 ml) at the most. I like to use wide-mouth jars; disposable wood cones, cups, and boats; glassware, including vintage glassware for special occasions; plastic cups; and mini boards. But the options are endless, depending on how creative you want to get. Most containers can be found at party supply stores, dollar stores, or online (see Resources on page 135).

SKEWERS, TOOTHPICKS, AND DECORATIVE PICKS

A large part of jarcuterie is assembling skewers of food not only to get all those delicious flavors into a single serving but also to create visual appeal through height. To achieve that, you'll want to have a good variety of skewers, toothpicks, and decorative picks in different sizes. I suggest using only ones made of wood or bamboo that are not too thick and often designated for appetizers. The most common sizes I use are 4 and 6 inches (10 and 15 cm) long. Here are the terms I use throughout the book and what they mean:

Round skewers: These are your basic wood skewers, which have a round body with one end flat and the other pointed.

Knotted or loop flat skewers: These skewers are made of bamboo and have a decorative knot or loop at one end. Instead of being round like regular skewers, they have a flat body, which works best for skewering cheeses but can hold other types of foods too.

Toothpicks: These are usually shorter in size, no longer than 4 inches (10 cm), and can be interchangeable with the term "skewers" when searching online. You may find some that are the same as the round skewers described above and others that have both ends pointed (these are sometimes called "cocktail sticks"). They both work.

Decorative picks: These are skewers/toothpicks that have a decorative element on them, like a colored ball, crystal cube, or themed shape. There are a lot of fun options out there, and they are a great way to elevate your jarcuterie for special occasions.

CUTTING BOARDS

I like to have several cutting boards on hand in assorted sizes. I use the larger ones for laying out ingredients to prep or assemble, and I use smaller ones to do the actual prep work, such as cutting ingredients.

PARING KNIFE

A very sharp paring knife is essential for cutting small, precise shapes.

CHEESE KNIFE

A good cheese knife with holes in the blade will help you cut cheese more smoothly. The holes keep cheese from sticking to the blade due to minimal surface-area contact. The holes also come in handy when the cheese does stick because you can push it off the knife through the holes.

CHEESE WIRE

This tool will make your life much easier! I rely on this daily to evenly slice cheese, especially soft and semisoft cheeses, such as fresh mozzarella and goat cheese.

WAVY CUTTER

This can also be called a crinkle cutter. You've probably seen it used for cutting french fries, but I have a small one that I often use for cutting fresh fruit or vegetables. It gives them some visual interest, but it also serves a purpose by helping keep dips from sliding off your veggies.

COOKIE CUTTERS

I have a growing collection of mini cookie cutters—1 to 2 inches (2.5 to 5 cm) in size—because they are a quick and easy way to add to a theme for a special occasion. I like to cut out shapes from fruit, vegetables, cheese, bread, cookies, and more.

SCOOP

My #100 scoop is truly one of my favorite kitchen tools. I use it for cheese truffles, chocolate truffles, mini cookies, and as a melon baller.

EDIBLE INK PEN

Keep a few of these in your kitchen and you will be surprised how often you use them. They are great for personalizing food with names or drawing eyes and faces onto food items. An edible ink pen is a simple way to make things more fun, especially for the kiddos!

THE GRAZE ANATOMY OF JARCUTERIE

Understanding the basic anatomy of jarcuterie will make it easier for you to create your own! There is a lot of flexibility in what you can use to build your own unique versions, and I've already gone through all the trial and error so you don't have to. Here are some basic elements that I've learned to include along the way.

HEIGHT

Adding components of varying height to your jarcuterie makes the presentation more appealing and allows people to really see everything in the container. A good place to start is to add something tall like a pretzel rod or breadstick, and then you can add more height with food on skewers and picks.

BASE

After adding the main height component, which is usually a pretzel rod or the like, you'll need something in the base. This helps stabilize everything and give it a visual foundation. I've found that foods like grapes, blueberries, and nuts work best. You want something that won't get soggy and will complement the other flavors in the jar. Avoid using crackers or fruit that is too moist.

SKEWERS AND PICKS

This is where you can get creative! For classic jarcuterie that is a spin-off of a charcuterie or grazing board, I like to add a skewer with savory meats, cheeses, olives, and pickles, and another skewer with fruit or fruit and cheese. Keep your skewers consistent with flavor profiles that make sense. Avoid pairing salami with berries or olives with fruit. You also want to think about the order people will consume each bite.

ADD-INS

These are bites that complement the skewers, such as crackers, a fresh veggie or two, a sweet bite, extra bites of cheeses, a honey straw or pipette, and so on, that are placed into the open spaces.

FILLERS

These are just what you'd think: bite-size components that help make the jar look full. You can sprinkle nuts, small berries, or sweet tidbits on top and to fill any gaps.

TOPPER

I love to include a topper of some sort and think of it as the cherry on top. I usually achieve this look with a cheese truffle for savory jarcuterie and a candy truffle for sweet jarcuterie.

GARNISH

Don't forget to add the garnish! This can be fresh herbs, edible flowers, or even a decorative pick. You can also add this element to the rim of the jar using fruit slices. The garnish completes the look and can even help tie your jarcuterie into a color scheme or theme.

GETTING STARTED

When thinking through the approach for your own jarcuterie, certain things will work better than others. Here are some of the tips and tricks I've learned that may help you.

CHEESES
Certain types of cheeses can be threaded onto skewers and picks easier than others. I've found that hard cheeses don't work well. If you try to thread hard Parmesan or extra-sharp cheddar onto a skewer, it will likely crumble and fall off. Stick with mild, soft, or semisoft cheeses. Mild cheddar, Havarti, mozzarella, Colby Jack, Monterey Jack, smoked Gouda, and Muenster are all good choices. I've also found that cheeses generally tend to work better on flat bamboo skewers rather than round ones because they are less likely to crack.

MEATS
There is a lot of flexibility when it comes to what meats you choose to use. I find it easiest to use presliced salami. You can find this in the lunch-meat section, or you can have it thinly sliced at the deli. The slices I use typically range anywhere from 2 to 3 inches (5 to 7.5 cm) in diameter. I like to fold smaller slices in half to put on picks and larger slices in quarters. You can also buy sticks of salami and slice it for the skewers. I haven't come across any particular style of salami that doesn't work. You can also use other deli meats such as pepperoni, chorizo, prosciutto, speck, turkey, chicken, roast beef, ham, and so on. These can be folded like salami, or larger pieces can be sliced into strips and threaded onto skewers ribbon style.

FRUITS AND VEGGIES
The first thing to do with fruits and veggies is to wash them properly. Then you will want to pat them dry with paper towels, which will help keep other components from getting soggy and prevent flavors from mixing. I love to use fresh fruit such as grapes, strawberries, blueberries, blackberries, raspberries, and figs. They are showy and taste delicious when paired with cheeses. Dried fruit is a great add-in as well—apricots, mango, and pineapple are good choices. Veggies that work well as add-ins include carrots, cucumbers, bell peppers, endive, broccolini, and snap peas. Cherry or grape tomatoes also make great additions to skewers and picks.

OLIVES AND PICKLES
As with fruits and veggies, you will want to pat dry pickles and olives with paper towels to help keep other components from getting soggy and flavors from mixing. When it comes to olives, use what you like. If you aren't sure, then start with Castelvetrano olives, also known as gateway olives. They are mild and buttery and have a nice meaty texture. Plus, their gorgeous bright-green hue will add visual appeal to your jarcuterie. As for pickles, again, use what you like. I regularly use cornichons, mini sweet or dill pickles, or pickled okra, and I occasionally use pickled asparagus or green beans to cover both the pickled aspect and the need for height. Anything pickled will complement traditional jarcuterie.

THREADING SKEWERS AND PICKS

I covered some of this already, but this is a reminder that not all cheeses work well threaded onto round skewers. Make sure to use flat skewers when appropriate, and reserve the round ones for items such as fruits, veggies, meats, and olives. Even pickles can split easily on round skewers. If you are unsure, test it out first. You don't want to deal with items breaking or falling off right before a party. Also, if you want a particular component, like a berry, to be the topper on a skewer, turn your skewer or pick with the pointed end up and thread the other skewer items first, followed by the berry (topper) last, making sure not to pierce through the top of the berry. If any of your skewers have the look you want but are too long, just clip them to the desired length with scissors or wire cutters for thicker ones.

SHOPPING

Once you decide on the ingredients you want to use, make a thorough shopping list. You can usually shop for items several days in advance, though some fresh fruit and veggies may need to be bought closer to the event. Storing these fresh ingredients in glass jars once you get home will help keep them fresh longer. Also, the main thing I have to stress when making your shopping plans is to do the math! Since jarcuterie is individual servings, this makes the math easy. You can calculate exactly how much of each ingredient will be needed so that you don't accidentally overbuy or underbuy.

PREP

Prep is the key to making jarcuterie easy and successful. Meats and cheeses can be cut and stored a day or two in advance. If your jarcuterie requires any fresh fruits and veggies to be cut, wait until the day you intend to serve it to prepare those ingredients. Most picks and skewers can be assembled the day before you serve. This can be super helpful and a time- and stress-saver the day of your event. I assemble skewers and then store them in airtight plastic containers with paper towels layered between levels of assembled skewers. This helps keep flavors and sometimes colors (from berries) from bleeding onto each other. Counting is a big part of prep. I find it helpful to count out each ingredient so that it is ready to go when you assemble the jars. You can have tomatoes, berries, grapes, cheese cubes, and most everything counted out in advance. For example, since it's tough to know how many grapes are in a bunch that you've purchased, it's important to wash, dry, and count them in advance so that you know you have enough. I'm always amazed at how much math is involved in jarcuterie! At least it's easy math, because ingredient measurements are pretty exact. The day you are serving the jarcuterie, you can assemble the jars 1 to 2 hours prior to the event. You don't want to do it much earlier than that because things like crackers will get soggy.

PACKAGING AND TRANSPORTING

This isn't as hard as it may seem! Jarcuterie is easy to package up and transport if you want to give it as a gift or take it to an event. One way to package it is to individually place each jarcuterie in a cellophane bag and tie it closed at the top with twine or ribbon. This method can be time consuming if you have a lot of containers, and it is unnecessary if you intend to just have the items displayed and ready to eat when you arrive at the venue. In that case, you can put your jarcuterie in cardboard trays or baker boxes with the lids cut off. Then, place the tray or box into a cellophane gift-basket bag and tape or tie it closed. These bags are larger cellophane bags that can be found in or near the gift-wrap section in stores. For information on how to transport cones, see page 25.

FOOD-STYLING TECHNIQUES

From cutting cheese cubes to creating a pepperoni rose, these are the techniques you will see throughout the book. If you are unsure how to prep an ingredient, refer back here to get it just right!

CHEESES

Chunk: Cut ¾ to 1 inch (2 to 5 cm) in size.

Cube: Cut ½ to ¾ inch (1 to 2 cm) in size (unless otherwise stated).

Slice: Cheese that you slice yourself from a block of cheese works best with cookie cutters rather than presliced or deli-sliced cheese. Use a cheese wire to cut the slices between ⅛ and ¼ inch (3 and 6 mm) thick.

Rosette (for provolone): Cut a thin round slice of provolone in half, and then roll each half fairly tightly from one end to the other into a rosette. Secure with a toothpick if desired.

Square: Cut ⅛ to ¼ inch (3 to 6 mm) thick and 1 inch (2.5 cm) square.

Triangle (for medium to hard cheeses): Cut ⅛ to ¼ inch (3 to 6 mm) thick and 1 inch (2.5 cm) wide at the top.

Wedge (for semisoft and soft cheeses): Cut ½ inch (1 cm) thick and 1 inch (2.5 cm) wide at the top.

MEATS

Quarter-folded (for salami): Fold a thin slice of salami in half and then in half again.

Ribbon-folded (for prosciutto): Lay out a slice of prosciutto and fold it in half lengthwise. Starting at one end, fold it in a back-and-forth wave pattern, with each wave about 1 inch (2.5 cm) wide. Secure with a toothpick if desired. Serve with the fatty (white) side of the ribbon at the top.

Rose (for pepperoni or salami): Using a small container (such as a 2-ounce portion cup), line the inside with four slices of pepperoni or salami, overlapping each slice just a bit. Then lay out four more slices of pepperoni or salami on a board, once again overlapping each slice just a bit. Collectively fold the slices in half horizontally, and then tightly roll from one end to the other. Once rolled, place in the middle of the meat-lined container with the folded side down. For fuller roses, use more slices.

Rosette (for salami or speck): Fold a thin slice of salami or speck in half, and then roll fairly tightly from one end to the other to form a rosette. Secure with a toothpick if desired.

VEGETABLES

Cucumber wedge: For a mini cucumber, slice off the ends, cut the cucumber in half horizontally, and then cut each half into four wedges. For a regular-size cucumber, slice off an end, and then cut a piece 3 to 4 inches (7.5 to 10 cm) in length. Cut that piece into four wedges.

Radish tulip: Trim the top and bottom ends off a radish, and then slice the radish in half lengthwise. Use a paring knife to cut a zigzag pattern across the top of a radish half, making three peaks with the middle one slightly taller than the other two.

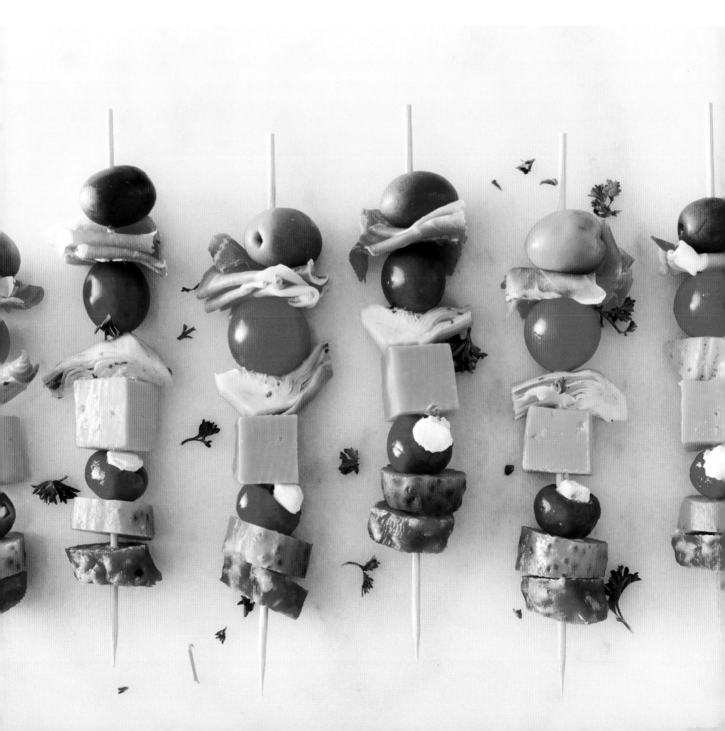

CLASSICS

mpress your guests with this new way of entertaining! In this chapter, I show you how to create jarcuterie that shares ingredients with traditional grazing boards. I have created some of these projects using jars, but I also use some of my other favorite containers, such as cones, mini boats, and mini boards. There are even some edible versions made with bread! Feel free to use what you have on hand or whatever creative container you can come up with. The ideas here are all great appetizers for cocktail and dinner parties.

CLASSIC JARCUTERIE

This is where my love for jarcuterie began! I created this grazing-style jar that embodies all the wonderful aspects of a charcuterie board but in a single serving. It's not only easy for guests to carry but also delicious and visually appealing.

MAKES 4 JARS

SUPPLIES
4 jars, 8 ounces (240 ml) in size
4 knotted flat skewers, 6 inches (15 cm) long
4 knotted flat skewers, 4 inches (10 cm) long
4 toothpicks, 4 inches (10 cm) long

SALAMI SKEWERS
4 pitted Castelvetrano olives
4 cubes mild cheddar cheese
4 slices regular salami, quarter-folded
4 grape or cherry tomatoes
4 slices spicy salami, quarter-folded

FRUIT SKEWERS
4 raspberries
4 grapes
4 blackberries

EVERYTHING BAGEL CHEESE TRUFFLE SKEWERS
4 Everything Bagel Cheese Truffles (see recipe on page 124)

ADDITIONAL INGREDIENTS
4 La Panzanella Mini Croccantini Artisan Crackers
4 pretzel rods
16 to 20 grapes
4 wedges cucumber
4 squares Havarti cheese
4 multigrain crackers (such as Crunchmaster Multi-Grain Baked Crackers)
4 triangles Manchego cheese
3 to 4 tablespoons (25 to 35 g) roasted almonds
4 to 8 sprigs fresh herbs, for garnishing

1. **To assemble the salami skewers:** Thread the 6-inch (15 cm) knotted skewers each with an olive, a cheddar cube, a quarter-folded slice of regular salami, a tomato, and a quarter-folded slice of spicy salami. Set aside.

2. **To assemble the fruit skewers:** Thread the 4-inch (10 cm) knotted skewers each with a raspberry, a grape, and a blackberry. Set aside.

3. **To assemble the everything bagel cheese truffle skewers:** Thread the 4-inch (10 cm) toothpicks each with an Everything Bagel Cheese Truffle. Set aside.

4. **To assemble the jars:** Place a La Panzanella cracker and a pretzel rod in the back of each jar, and then add four or five grapes to the base.

5. Insert a salami skewer in the back right and a fruit skewer in the back left.

6. Place the cucumber wedge at an angle in front of the salami skewer and the Manchego triangle, with the point down, behind the fruit skewer.

7. Place a Havarti square in the front left and a multigrain cracker in the front middle.

8. Place an everything bagel cheese truffle skewer in the middle on top.

9. Fill in gaps with the roasted almonds and garnish with the fresh herbs.

MINI JARCUTERIE

This mini version of my Classic Jarcuterie (page 21) is the perfect portion for any gathering where guests will be mingling for a shorter amount of time, such as a quick cocktail hour or an appetizer course at a dinner party.

This mini version of my Classic Jarcuterie (page 21)

MAKES 6 MINI JARS

SUPPLIES

6 jars, 4 ounces (120 ml) in size

6 knotted flat skewers, 6 inches (15 cm) long

6 knotted flat skewers, 4 inches (10 cm) long

6 toothpicks, 4 inches (10 cm) long

SALAMI SKEWERS

6 pitted Castelvetrano olives

18 slices regular salami, quarter-folded

FRUIT SKEWERS

6 blueberries

6 raspberries

6 cubes Havarti

EVERYTHING BAGEL CHEESE TRUFFLE SKEWERS

6 Everything Bagel Cheese Truffles (see recipe on page 124)

6 grape or cherry tomatoes

ADDITIONAL INGREDIENTS

12 La Panzanella Mini Croccantini Artisan Crackers

6 pretzel rods

1½ cups (225 g) blueberries

6 triangles smoked Gouda cheese

6 slices spicy salami, rolled into rosettes

6 sprigs fresh herbs, for garnishing

1. **To assemble the salami skewers:** Thread the 6-inch (15 cm) knotted skewers each with an olive and three quarter-folded slices of regular salami. Set aside.

2. **To assemble the fruit skewers:** Thread the 4-inch knotted skewers each with a blueberry, a raspberry, and a Havarti cube. Set aside.

3. **To assemble the everything bagel cheese truffle skewers:** Thread the 4-inch (10 cm) toothpicks each with an Everything Bagel Cheese Truffle and a tomato. Set aside.

4. **To assemble the jars:** Place a La Panzanella cracker and a pretzel rod in the back of each jar, and then pour ¼ cup (38 g) of the blueberries into the base. Place a second cracker in the back.

5. Insert a salami skewer in the right side, a fruit skewer in the left side, and an everything bagel cheese truffle skewer in the middle.

6. Place a Gouda triangle, with the point up, in the front right and a salami rosette in the front middle.

7. Garnish with a sprig of fresh herbs.

GRAZING CONES

Grazing cones have a cute and unique look that always delights guests, and they are easy to assemble because the shape of the cone helps hold everything in place. Made with eco-friendly wood, these disposable cones allow for a quick cleanup. It doesn't get better than that!

Here are a few ways to hold and display the cones:

- You can turn a wire basket upside down and insert the cones into the spaces between the wires (as pictured). You can even decorate the basket with fresh herbs, eucalyptus, and food-safe flowers for a stunning display piece.

- Another way to display and transport cones is to use a six-pack bottle carrier. You can upcycle one or order plain ones online. This also makes a cute presentation for gift giving. The larger cones fit perfectly into each slot. Sometimes I elevate them by wadding up a piece of tissue paper into the base of each slot, which helps secure the base from sliding around too much and makes it easier to get them out of the carrier. If transporting, once the cones are in a carrier, you can use a cellophane gift-basket bag to wrap them up and tie closed with twine or ribbon.

- If you are really committed to serving grazing cones, you can purchase a cone display made of wood, metal, or plastic.

- If you don't have any of the above options, you can lean the cones upright inside a regular basket or carefully lay the cones on a platter or board.

CLASSIC GRAZING CONES

These cones resemble my Classic Jarcuterie (page 21). Your guests will be surprised by how many of their favorite ingredients you were able to easily fit inside these cones!

MAKES 6 CONES

SUPPLIES

6 disposable wood cones, 7.1 inches (18 cm) tall

6 loop or knotted flat skewers, 6 inches (15 cm) long

12 knotted flat skewers, 4 inches (10 cm) long, divided

SALAMI SKEWERS

6 grape or cherry tomatoes

6 petite dill or sweet pickles

6 cubes mild cheddar cheese

6 slices spicy salami, quarter-folded

6 slices regular salami, quarter-folded

BLACKBERRY SKEWERS

6 blackberries

6 cubes Havarti cheese

6 raspberries

BLUEBERRY SKEWERS

24 to 30 blueberries

ADDITIONAL INGREDIENTS

6 pretzel rods

18 to 24 grapes

6 wedges cucumber

12 multigrain crackers (such as Crunchmaster Multi-Grain Baked Crackers)

12 slices regular salami, rolled into rosettes (use 2 slices per rosette)

6 triangles Manchego cheese

6 sprigs fresh herbs, for garnishing

1. **To assemble the salami skewers:** Thread the six 6-inch (15 cm) loop skewers each with a tomato, a pickle, a cheddar cube, a quarter-folded slice of spicy salami, and a quarter-folded slice of regular salami. Set aside.

2. **To assemble the blackberry skewers:** Thread six 4-inch (10 cm) knotted skewers each with a blackberry, a Havarti cube, and a raspberry. Set aside.

3. **To assemble the blueberry skewers:** Thread the remaining six 4-inch (10 cm) knotted skewers each with four or five blueberries. Set aside.

4. **To assemble the cones:** Place the cones upright in a holder. Lean a pretzel rod in the back of each cone, followed by three or four grapes in the base.

5. Insert a salami skewer in the right side, a blackberry skewer to the left of the pretzel rod, and a blueberry skewer in the left side.

6. Place a cucumber wedge in front of the salami skewer and two multigrain crackers in front of the blackberry skewer.

7. Place a salami rosette in the front middle.

8. Insert a Manchego triangle, with the point down, in the back of the cone.

9. Garnish with a sprig of fresh herbs.

VEGETARIAN GRAZING CONES

Vegetarian cones are a safe bet when you don't know your guests' dietary preferences and are a good grazing choice for any gathering. I promise that no one will miss the meat!

MAKES 4 CONES

SUPPLIES

4 disposable wood cones, 7.1 inches (18 cm) tall

4 loop or knotted flat skewers, 6 inches (15 cm) long

4 knotted flat skewers, 4 inches (10 cm) long

4 round skewers, 6 inches (15 cm) long

4 toothpicks, 4 inches (10 cm) long

SAVORY SKEWERS

4 grape tomatoes

4 cubes mild cheddar cheese

4 petite dill pickles

4 cubes Colby Jack cheese

FRUIT SKEWERS

4 blackberries

4 cubes Havarti cheese

4 grapes

BLUEBERRY SKEWERS

24 blueberries

EVERYTHING BAGEL CHEESE TRUFFLE SKEWERS

4 Everything Bagel Cheese Truffles (see recipe on page 124)

ADDITIONAL INGREDIENTS

4 flatbread crackers

4 pretzel rods

20 to 24 grapes

4 wedges cucumber

4 slices provolone cheese, rolled into rosettes

20 to 24 pea crisps

4 sprigs fresh herbs, for garnishing

1. **To assemble the savory skewers:** Thread the 6-inch (15 cm) loop skewers each with a tomato, a cheddar cube, a pickle, and a Colby Jack cube. Set aside.

2. **To assemble the fruit skewers:** Thread the 4-inch (10 cm) knotted skewers each with a blackberry, a Havarti cube, and a grape. Set aside.

3. **To assemble the blueberry skewers:** Thread the 6-inch (15 cm) round skewers each with six blueberries. Set aside.

4. **To assemble the everything bagel cheese truffle skewers:** Thread the 4-inch (10 cm) toothpicks each with an Everything Bagel Cheese Truffle. Set aside.

5. **To assemble the cones:** Place the cones upright in a holder. Lean a flatbread cracker and a pretzel rod in the back of each cone, and then add four or five grapes to the base.

6. Place a savory skewer in the right side, a fruit skewer in the left side, and a blueberry skewer in front of the flatbread cracker.

7. Insert a cucumber wedge between the blueberry and fruit skewers.

8. Place an everything bagel cheese truffle skewer in the middle on top.

9. Place a provolone rosette in the front right, and then fill in gaps around the rosette and cheese truffle skewer with five or six of the pea crisps.

10. Garnish with a sprig of fresh herbs.

VEGAN GRAZING CONES

Vegans don't have to miss out on anything when it comes to grazing! With delicious vegan cheeses paired with healthy fruits and veggies, these cones prove that you won't miss the meat and dairy.

MAKES 6 CONES

SUPPLIES

6 disposable wood cones, 7.1 inches (18 cm) tall

6 loop or knotted flat skewers, 6 inches (15 cm) long

6 knotted flat skewers, 4 inches (10 cm) long

TOMATO-CUCUMBER SKEWERS

6 grape or cherry tomatoes

6 cubes vegan cheese

6 mini cucumber slices, cut with a wavy cutter

TOMATO-OLIVE SKEWERS

6 pitted Castelvetrano olives

6 cubes vegan cheese of choice

6 grape or cherry tomatoes

ADDITIONAL INGREDIENTS

18 to 24 grapes

6 wedges cucumber

6 baby carrots, cut in half lengthwise

6 wedges soft vegan cheese (such as Miyoko's Double Cream Classic Chive)

12 to 15 fruit-and-nut crisps (such as Lesley Stowe Raincoast Crisps)

3 mini peppers, cut in half lengthwise and seeded

⅓ to ½ cup (45 to 70 g) roasted almonds

18 to 30 blueberries

6 sprigs fresh herbs, for garnishing

1. **To assemble the tomato-cucumber skewers:** Thread the 6-inch (15 cm) loop skewers each with a tomato, a cheese cube, and a cucumber slice. Set aside.

2. **To assemble the tomato-olive skewers:** Thread the 4-inch (10 cm) knotted skewers each with an olive, a cheese cube, and a tomato. Set aside.

3. **To assemble the cones:** Place the cones upright in a holder. Add three or four grapes to the base of each cone.

4. Insert a tomato-cucumber skewer in the right side and a tomato-olive skewer in the left side.

5. Place a cucumber wedge in front of the tomato-olive skewer, two carrot halves in front of the tomato-cucumber skewer, and a soft cheese wedge next to the cucumber wedge.

6. Insert two or three fruit-and-nut crisps in the back middle, and then place a mini pepper half in front of the crackers.

7. Fill in gaps with the roasted almonds and three to five blueberries.

8. Garnish with a sprig of fresh herbs.

PERSONAL CHARCUTERIE BOARDS

I adore these mini charcuterie boards! They are a great start to any dinner party, and the crackers with your guests' names written on them in edible ink can also act as place cards.

MAKES 6 MINI BOARDS

SUPPLIES

6 disposable mini wood boards, 5 x 5 inches (12.5 x 12.5 cm) in size (excluding the handle)

Edible ink pen

INGREDIENTS

6 La Panzanella Mini Croccantini Artisan Crackers (or sourdough flatbread crackers)

12 fruit-and-nut crisps (such as Lesley Stowe Raincoast Crisps)

12 dried apricots

12 wedges Brie cheese

6 small bunches grapes

18 slices salami, folded in half

18 squares aged white cheddar cheese

12 slices hot soppressata or chorizo

42 to 48 toasted walnuts

54 to 60 blueberries

6 to 12 sprigs fresh herbs, for garnishing

 TIP JAR

Assemble these mini boards at each place setting so that you don't have to move them later.

1. Write your guests' names on the La Panzanella crackers with the edible ink pen. Set aside.

2. **To assemble the mini boards:** Place two fruit-and-nut crisps and two dried apricots on the back left of each board.

3. Place two Brie wedges on the back right and a small bunch of grapes in the back middle.

4. Lean a cracker with a name written on it at a slight angle against the items on the back of the board, making it the centerpiece.

5. Working clockwise from the right side of the centerpiece, place three folded slices of salami, three cheddar squares, two slices of soppressata, seven or eight walnuts, and nine or ten blueberries.

6. Garnish with a sprig or two of fresh herbs.

MELON CAPRESE MINI BOATS

These eco-friendly, disposable mini boats are a versatile option for individual grazing. I like to use them for serving traditional charcuterie snacks, as well as these colorful melon caprese skewers full of fresh flavors.

MAKES 12 MINI BOATS

SUPPLIES

12 disposable mini wood boats, 4.3 to 5.5 inches (11 to 14 cm) long

#100 scoop or melon baller

24 decorative skewers, 4 inches (10 cm) long

INGREDIENTS

1 small watermelon

1 small cantaloupe

1 small honeydew

12 blackberries

24 bocconcini (mini mozzarella balls)

48 leaves fresh basil

12 slices prosciutto, folded in ribbons

Balsamic glaze, for drizzling

 TIP JAR

To add even more color to these caprese boats, line each boat with a piece of red cabbage before adding the prosciutto ribbons and skewers.

1. Scoop out six balls each from the watermelon, cantaloupe, and honeydew with the scoop or melon baller for a total of eighteen balls. Then cut six 1-inch (2.5 cm) cubes from each melon for a total of eighteen cubes.

2. **To assemble the skewers:** Thread each skewer following these guidelines to get a variety of skewers.

   - Each skewer should have two different types of fruit (blackberry, watermelon, cantaloupe, honeydew). If placing two melon pieces on the same skewer, make sure one is a ball and the other is a cube.

   - Each skewer should have a bocconcino.

   - Each skewer should have two basil leaves inserted between the ingredients. If a basil leaf is large, fold it in half or quarters first.

   - Thread the two pieces of fruit and bocconcino on each skewer in any order you like, making sure to insert basil leaves between ingredients.

3. **To assemble the boats:** Place a prosciutto ribbon diagonally in each boat at one end, and then lay two skewers diagonally across each boat. You want the four fruit pieces on the two skewers in each boat to be comprised of each type of fruit: blackberry, watermelon, cantaloupe, and honeydew. If the skewers were assembled per the guidelines in step 2, you should be able to achieve this.

4. Drizzle the skewers with the balsamic glaze.

CHARCUTERIE KEBABS

If you can think of an occasion, then you have an excuse to make these kebabs! With a bite of everything found on a grazing board assembled on a portable skewer, these kebabs can come together at the last minute.

MAKES 12 KEBABS

SUPPLIES

12 round skewers, 12 inches (30.5 cm) long

INGREDIENTS

12 grapes

12 dried apricots

6 mini Brie rounds, 0.9 ounce (25 g) in size, cut in half

12 strawberries

12 cubes Havarti cheese, 1 inch (2.5 cm) in size

24 leaves fresh basil

24 slices regular salami, quarter-folded

24 slices spicy salami, quarter-folded

24 chunks bread of choice, 1 inch (2.5 cm) in size

12 cubes Colby Jack cheese, 1 inch (2.5 cm) in size

12 petite dill or sweet pickles

12 pitted Castelvetrano olives

TIP JAR

Serve the skewers on a large platter or board to make them visually appealing and easy to grab and go.

1. **To assemble the kebabs:** Thread the skewers each with a grape and pull it down the skewer, leaving about 1¾ to 2 inches (4.5 to 5 cm) at the bottom of the skewer for holding.

2. Thread a dried apricot onto the skewer and pull it all the way down to the grape.

3. Thread a mini Brie half onto the skewer, followed by a strawberry.

4. Add a Havarti cube, followed by a basil leaf. If the leaf is small, place as is; if the leaf is large, fold it in half or quarters first.

5. Thread a quarter-folded slice of regular salami followed by a quarter-folded slice of spicy salami onto the skewer.

6. Add a bread chunk, followed by a cube of Colby Jack and another basil leaf.

7. Add another quarter-folded slice of regular salami, followed by another quarter-folded slice of spicy salami.

8. Add a pickle and another chunk of bread.

9. Top with an olive.

EDIBLE BOARD CROSTINI

This is a cute and simple spin on mini charcuterie boards! Each crostino is made using a slice of bread cut into the shape of a board, which is then toasted and topped with one of three delicious toppings.

MAKES 12 CROSTINI (4 OF EACH TOPPING)

EDIBLE BOARDS: 12 slices bread, cut into mini board shapes (see Tip Jar on page 40) and toasted

TOPPING 1

20 to 30 grape or cherry tomatoes

Olive oil, to taste

Sea salt, to taste

4 tablespoons pesto

4 slices fresh mozzarella cheese

Balsamic glaze, for drizzling

12 leaves fresh basil

1. Preheat the oven to 450°F (230°C; gas mark 8).

2. Place the tomatoes in an oven-safe dish, drizzle with the olive oil, and sprinkle with the sea salt. Bake for 5 to 6 minutes. Remove from the oven and let cool.

3. **To assemble the crostini:** Lay out four edible boards. Spread each one with 1 tablespoon of the pesto. Place a slice of mozzarella on each board, and then top with four or five roasted tomatoes.

4. Drizzle with the balsamic glaze and garnish with three basil leaves.

TOPPING 2

12 fresh cherries, cut in half and pits removed

Olive oil, to taste

8 thin slices honey goat cheese

4 slices prosciutto, folded into ribbons

2 tablespoons chopped pistachios

Fresh cracked black pepper, to taste

1. Preheat the oven to 450°F (230°C; gas mark 8).

2. Place the cherry halves in an oven-safe dish and drizzle with the olive oil. Bake for 5 to 6 minutes. Remove from the oven and let cool.

3. **To assemble the crostini:** Lay out four edible boards. Place two slices of the honey goat cheese on each one, leaving space for a prosciutto ribbon on the top-right or top-left corner (depending which way the handle of the board is facing).

4. Place a prosciutto ribbon on the reserved space.

5. Top each board with six roasted cherry halves and the chopped pistachios.

6. Sprinkle with cracked pepper.

(continued)

TOPPING 3

4 slices speck or salami, folded into rosettes

20 to 28 leaves arugula

2 dried figs, cut in half

8 chunks blue cheese

8 tablespoons chopped toasted walnuts

Fresh cracked black pepper, to taste

🫙 TIP JAR

You can cut out the bread slices into a board shape with a knife, or you can get a custom cookie cutter made in the shape of a mini board like I did (see Resources on page 135).

1. **To assemble the crostini:** Lay out four edible boards. Place a speck rosette on the top-right or top-left corner (depending which way the handle of the board is facing) of each board.

2. Cover the rest of each board with five to seven arugula leaves.

3. Place a fig half on one of the lower corners, and then fill the two empty corners with a chunk of blue cheese.

4. Fill in gaps with 2 tablespoons of the chopped walnuts.

5. Sprinkle with the cracked pepper.

TIDBIT WINE TOPPERS

These wine-topper plates are perfectly sized to hold a tasty appetizer pairing while guests mingle. And bonus, if you're outside, the plate keeps bugs out of your wine! This project is for one pairing each, but you can easily multiply quantities and make as many as needed fairly quickly.

MAKES 4 PAIRINGS (1 OF EACH PAIRING)

SUPPLIES: 4 round wine-topper plates, about 4 inches (10 cm) in diameter

PAIRING 1

2 fruit-and-nut crisps (such as Lesley Stowe Raincoast Crisps)

1 slice prosciutto, folded into ribbons

2 wedges Brie cheese

3 thin slices Granny Smith apple

1 small sprig fresh rosemary, for garnishing

1. Place the fruit-and-nut crisps on the back middle of a wine-topper plate.

2. Place the prosciutto ribbon in front of the crisps, the Brie wedges on the right side, and the apple slices on the left side.

3. Garnish with the sprig of fresh rosemary.

PAIRING 2

1 small bunch grapes

1 or 2 mini toasts

6 toasted walnuts

1 chunk blue cheese

2 dried apricots

Honey, for drizzling

1. Place the bunch of grapes on the back middle of a wine-topper plate.

2. Working your way around the plate clockwise from the grapes, place the mini toast(s), the toasted walnuts, the blue cheese, and the dried apricots.

3. Drizzle the honey over everything on the plate except the grapes.

(continued)

PAIRING 3

2 triangles aged Gouda cheese

4 herb flatbread crackers

5 blackberries

3 slices speck or salami, rolled into rosettes

1 sprig fresh thyme, for garnishing

1. Place the Gouda triangles on the right side of a wine-topper plate and the crackers on the left.

2. Fill in the middle of the plate with the blackberries and place the salami rosettes between the Gouda and blackberries.

3. Garnish with the sprig of fresh thyme.

PAIRING 4 (NOT PICTURED)

2 toothpicks, 4 inches (10 cm) long

1 strip strawberry fruit leather, cut in half lengthwise

2 triangles Manchego cheese

3 slices smoked chorizo

3 multigrain crackers (such as Crunchmaster Multi-Grain Baked Crackers)

1 or 2 sprigs fresh oregano, for garnishing

1. Thread the 4-inch (10 cm) toothpicks each with a strip of strawberry fruit leather in a wave pattern. Set aside.

2. Place the Manchego triangles on the back middle of a wine-topper plate.

3. Working your way around the plate clockwise from the cheese, place the chorizo, the crackers, and the fruit leather skewers.

4. Garnish with a sprig or two of fresh oregano.

SIDECAR CHARCUTERIE CONES

These mini cones are the most adorable and tastiest wineglass accessories! This ingenious presentation may just upstage the delicious snacks, and your guests will be relieved to not have to juggle a glass and a plate.

MAKES 8 MINI CONES

SUPPLIES

8 disposable mini wood cones, 5.1 inches (13 cm) tall

8 regular-size clothespins

8 wineglasses

16 toothpicks, 4 inches (10 cm) long, divided

SALAMI SKEWERS

8 pitted Castelvetrano olives

24 slices salami, quarter-folded

GRAPE SKEWERS

16 to 24 grapes

ADDITIONAL INGREDIENTS

8 tablespoons roasted almonds

4 flatbread crackers, broken in half

8 triangles aged white cheddar cheese

16 slices extra-sharp cheddar cheese

8 sprigs fresh herbs, for garnishing

 TIP JAR

You can pour the wine into the glasses before or after you assemble the cones. In order to prevent the glasses from tipping over while assembling the cones, adding the wine first will give the glasses some weight.

1. Clip a cone to each wineglass with a clothespin (see Tip Jar below). Set aside.

2. **Assemble the salami skewers:** Thread eight toothpicks each with an olive and three quarter-folded slices of salami. Set aside.

3. **Assemble the grape skewers:** Thread the remaining eight toothpicks each with two or three grapes. Set aside.

4. **Assemble the cones:** Pour 1 tablespoon of the almonds into the base of each cone, and then place a flatbread cracker half in the back middle.

5. Insert a salami skewer in the right side and a grape skewer to the left of it.

6. Place a cheddar triangle, with the point up, to the left of the flatbread cracker and two slices of white cheddar in the front of each cone.

7. Garnish with a sprig of fresh herbs.

CRUDITÉS DIP CUPS

Not your ordinary crudités, this rainbow of veggies is served in a thick slice of baguette with the dip inside! Customize them with your favorite dip and veggies for any get-together or a clever way to get your kids to eat more vegetables.

SUPPLIES

12 toothpicks, 4 inches (10 cm) long, divided

DIP CUPS

1 sturdy standard baguette

GRAPE TOMATO SKEWERS

12 grape tomatoes

TULIP RADISH SKEWERS

3 radishes, cut in half and shaped into 6 tulips

ADDITIONAL INGREDIENTS

12 tablespoons vegetable dip of choice

6 pieces green leaf lettuce

6 celery sticks, ½ inch (1 cm) wide by 5 inches (12.5 cm) long

6 wedges cucumber

6 to 12 strips red bell pepper, ½ inch (1 cm) wide by 3 to 4 inches (7.5 to 10 cm) long

6 baby carrots, cut in half lengthwise

6 strips red onion, ½ inch (1 cm) wide by 3 to 4 inches (7.5 to 10 cm) long

6 snap peas

6 sprigs fresh parsley, for garnishing

TIP JAR

The tulip radishes can also go skewerless and be placed in the front middle of each dip cup.

1. **To make the dip cups:** Slice the baguette into 6 slices, each 2½ inches (6.5 cm) wide. Stand up the baguette slices and cut across the middle of each one about ½ inch (1 cm) deep. Slice off a semicircle from the top, creating a cup with a back rim. Remove 2 inches (5 cm) from the center of each baguette slice, leaving the bottom intact. Set aside.

2. **To assemble the grape tomato skewers:** Thread six toothpicks each with two grape tomatoes. Set aside.

3. **To assemble the tulip radish skewers:** Thread the remaining six toothpicks each with a tulip radish. Set aside.

4. **To assemble the dip cups:** Add 2 tablespoons of the vegetable dip to each cup, and then line the back of each cup with a piece of lettuce.

5. Insert a grape tomato skewer, tulip radish skewer, celery stick, cucumber wedge, one or two red bell pepper strips, two carrot halves, a red onion strip, and a snap pea into each baguette slice. Vary the heights of the vegetables and alternate colors for visual appeal.

6. Garnish with a sprig of fresh parsley.

HOLIDAYS

Start new holiday traditions with jarcuterie! In this chapter, I show you how easily customizable jarcuterie is to make every holiday extra festive. Using color schemes, mini cookie cutters, and specialty food items, along with playful containers, the creative options are endless. These projects are not only perfect for entertaining but they also make great gifts.

VALENTINE'S DAY CHOCOLATE CUPS

Surprise the loved ones in your life with these Valentine's Day sweet treats! They also make a great gift for a teacher, neighbor, or friend. Just slip the finished jars into plastic party-favor bags and tie closed with a cute ribbon.

MAKES 4 JARS

SUPPLIES

4 glasses or jars, 7 to 8 ounces (210 to 240 ml) in size

Mini heart-shaped cookie cutter

4 round skewers, 6 inches (15 cm) long

4 heart-shaped flat bamboo skewers, 4 inches (10 cm) long

4 toothpicks, 4 inches (10 cm) long

POUND CAKE SKEWERS

8 slices pound cake, cut ½ inch (1 cm) thick (for cookie cutter)

8 blueberries

STRAWBERRY SKEWERS

4 strawberries, tops removed and cut in half lengthwise

MARSHMALLOW SKEWERS

12 pink heart-shaped marshmallows (such as Lucky Charms Magically Delicious Marshmallows)

ADDITIONAL INGREDIENTS

8 tablespoons chocolate syrup (store-bought or see recipe on page 134)

4 pretzel rods

8 strawberry wafer cookies

8 heart-shaped cookies with jam filling

8 Strawberry Pocky

1. **To assemble the pound cake skewers:** Cut out eight heart shapes from the pound cake slices with the cookie cutter.

2. Thread the 6-inch (15 cm) round skewers each with a pound cake heart, a blueberry, another pound cake heart, and another blueberry. Set aside.

3. **To assemble the strawberry skewers:** Slice the tops of the strawberry halves into a rounded heart shape with a paring knife.

4. Thread the 4-inch (10 cm) heart-shaped skewers each with two strawberry hearts. Set aside.

5. **To assemble the marshmallow skewers:** Thread the 4-inch (10 cm) toothpicks each with three heart-shaped marshmallows. Set aside.

6. **To assemble the cups:** Pour 2 tablespoons of the chocolate syrup into each glass. Place a pretzel rod in the back, leaning it to the right.

7. Insert a pound cake skewer in the right side of each glass, a strawberry skewer in the left side, and a marshmallow skewer in front of the strawberry skewer.

8. Place two strawberry wafer cookies in the middle back.

9. Place two heart-shaped cookies in the middle, propping them up with the items behind them.

10. Stick two Pocky in the back on either side of the wafer cookies.

SAINT PATRICK'S DAY LᵁCKY JARS

Share a little luck of the Irish with these sweet jars! Easy to assemble and filled with green and rainbow candies, these jars may even outshine that pot o' gold.

SUPPLIES

4 jars, 4 ounces (120 ml) in size

16 decorative picks, 4 inches (10 cm) long, divided

CANDY SKEWERS

4 sour-apple gummy belts

4 rainbow gummy belts

16 green DOTS Gumdrops

MARSHMALLOW SKEWERS

8 clover-shaped marshmallows (such as Lucky Charms Magically Delicious Marshmallows)

ADDITIONAL INGREDIENTS

4 Sour Apple SweeTARTS Ropes

4 green-apple licorice twists

4 green rock candy sticks

1 bag Family-Size Original Skittles, 27.5 ounces (779 g) in size

1. **To assemble the candy skewers:** Thread four decorative picks each with a sour-apple gummy belt in a wave pattern and four decorative picks each with a rainbow belt in a wave pattern. Set aside.

2. Thread four decorative picks each with four DOTS Gumdrops, avoiding piercing through the top gumdrop. Set aside.

3. **To assemble the marshmallow skewers:** Holding the pointed ends up, thread the remaining four decorative picks each with two clover-shaped marshmallows, avoiding piercing through the top marshmallow. Set aside.

4. **To assemble the jars:** Place a SweeTARTS Rope in the back right of each jar, a licorice twist in the back left, and a rock candy stick in the back middle.

5. Fill each jar a little more than halfway full of Skittles.

6. Insert a sour-apple gummy belt skewer in the right side and a rainbow gummy belt skewer in the left side. Prop up these skewers using the Skittles to give them some extra height.

7. Insert a marshmallow skewer in the middle and a DOTS skewer at an angle in the front.

EASTER EGG TREAT CARTONS

This egg carton is too easy and too cute not to give it a try! You can swap out ingredients based on preferences, but I like to include a balance of sweet and savory treats. Get creative with your egg cartons by personalizing them.

MAKES 4 EGG CARTONS

SUPPLIES

4 brand-new paper egg cartons, for a dozen eggs (see Tip Jar below)

Mini bunny-shaped cookie cutter

Variety of mini flower-shaped cookie cutters

INGREDIENTS

8 slices white cheddar cheese (for cookie cutter)

8 slices orange cheddar cheese (for cookie cutter)

1 package edible Easter grass

8 baby carrots, cut in half lengthwise

8 grape tomatoes

12 small foil-wrapped chocolate bunnies

4 small bunches grapes

4 tablespoons Annie's Organic Cheddar Bunnies Baked Snack Crackers

16 to 20 foil-wrapped chocolate mini eggs

4 tablespoons jelly beans

32 slices pepperoni, folded into 4 roses (8 slices per rose)

4 strawberries

32 blueberries

4 Peeps Marshmallow Chicks

1. Cut out four bunny shapes and four mini flower shapes from the white cheddar slices and eight mini flower shapes from the orange cheddar slices with the cookie cutters. Set aside.

2. **To assemble the egg cartons:** Spread the edible grass around the compartments of each egg carton.

3. Working from the back left to the back right of each carton, fill the compartments with four carrot halves and two tomatoes, three chocolate bunnies, a bunch of grapes, a tablespoon of Cheddar Bunnies, and four or five chocolate mini eggs.

4. Working from the front left to the front right of each carton, fill the compartments with a tablespoon of jelly beans; a pepperoni rose; a white cheddar bunny, a white cheddar flower, and two orange cheddar flowers; a strawberry and eight blueberries; and a marshmallow chick.

 TIP JAR

You must use brand-new egg cartons for this project, as an egg carton that has contained eggs could carry a risk of cross contamination.

MOTHER'S DAY TEACUPS

These teacup treats are fit for a queen—mom! Beautiful vintage teacups and saucers make the perfect backdrop for this elegant finger food. They're also perfect for afternoon tea parties and baby and bridal showers.

MAKES 4 TEACUPS

SUPPLIES
4 teacups and saucers
4 toothpicks, 4 inches (10 cm) long

CHICKEN SALAD–STUFFED CELERY
4 celery ribs, cut 6 inches (15 cm) long
12 to 16 ounces (340 to 454 g) chicken salad

FLORAL CHEESE TRUFFLE SKEWERS
4 Floral Cheese Truffles (see recipe on page 125)

ADDITIONAL INGREDIENTS
4 rolled wafer cookies
1 cup (150 g) blueberries
4 or 8 Cucumber Canapés (see recipe on page 129)
4 shortbread cookies (such as Walkers brand)
12 strawberries, 4 sliced ¾ inch (2 cm) from the base and 8 left whole, divided
12 to 16 blackberries
12 raspberries
4 small bunches grapes
4 sprigs fresh herbs, for garnishing

 TIP JAR

I love using vintage teacups and saucers for this project. If you don't have any on hand, thrift stores can be a great resource for finding some at a reasonable price. And they don't all have to match! Mismatched vintage pieces can add extra charm to any occasion.

1. **To assemble the chicken salad–stuffed celery:** Fill each celery rib with some chicken salad, leaving about one-quarter of the rib empty at the base. Set aside.

2. **To assemble the floral cheese truffle skewers:** Thread each toothpick with a Floral Cheese Truffle. Set aside.

3. **To assemble the teacups:** Place a chicken salad–stuffed piece of celery in the back middle of each teacup.

4. Place a rolled wafer cookie to the left of the celery, and then pour ¼ cup (38 g) of the blueberries into the base of each teacup.

5. Place one or two Cucumber Canapés to the right of the celery, a shortbread cookie to the left of the rolled wafer cookie, and a slit strawberry on the teacup's rim next to the shortbread cookie.

6. Insert a floral cheese truffle skewer in the middle of each teacup.

7. Place three or four blackberries and three raspberries around the cheese truffle skewer.

8. Place a small bunch of grapes on the saucer to the left of the cup and two whole strawberries to the right of the cup.

9. Garnish with a sprig of fresh herbs.

FATHER'S DAY GRAZING CUPS

Dad is sure to love this grazing cup filled to the brim with his favorite treats! It takes sweet and salty to a new level with candied bacon, cheeses, nuts, chocolate, and more. Even though these cups are designed with Dad in mind, the whole family is sure to love them.

MAKES 4 CUPS

SUPPLIES

4 disposable slanted wood cups, 6 ounces (180 ml) in size

Mini fluted round cookie cutter

4 knotted flat skewers, 6 inches (15 cm) long

4 round skewers, 6 inches (15 cm) long

8 toothpicks, 4 inches (10 cm) long, divided

SALAMI SKEWERS

24 thin slices smoked cheddar (for cookie cutter)

4 cubes pepper jack cheese

24 thin slices peppered salami

PEANUT BUTTER CUP SKEWERS

16 milk chocolate mini peanut butter cups

16 white chocolate mini peanut butter cups

16 dark chocolate mini peanut butter cups

DILL PICKLE SKEWERS

4 petite dill pickles

EVERYTHING BAGEL CHEESE TRUFFLE SKEWERS

4 Everything Bagel Cheese Truffles (see recipe on page 124)

ADDITIONAL INGREDIENTS

8 pieces Candied Bacon Strips (see recipe on page 128)

4 pretzel rods

1 cup (140 g) smoked almonds

48 to 60 small cheese crackers (such as Cheez-It brand)

8 triangles aged Gouda cheese

4 sprigs fresh rosemary, for garnishing

1. **To assemble the salami skewers:** Cut out twenty-four fluted round shapes from the smoked cheddar slices with the cookie cutter.

2. Thread the four 6-inch (15 cm) knotted bamboo skewers each with a pepper jack cube, two peppered salami slices, two smoked cheddar rounds, two more slices of peppered salami, two more slices of smoked cheddar, the remaining two slices of peppered salami, and the remaining two slices of smoked cheddar. Set aside.

3. **To assemble the peanut butter cup skewers:** Thread the four 6-inch round skewers each with a milk chocolate peanut butter cup, a white chocolate peanut butter cup, and a dark chocolate peanut butter cup. Set aside.

4. **To assemble the dill pickle skewers:** Thread four 4-inch (10 cm) toothpicks each with a petite dill pickle. Set aside.

5. **To assemble the everything bagel cheese truffle skewers:** Thread the remaining four 4-inch (10 cm) toothpicks each with an Everything Bagel Cheese Truffle. Set aside.

6. **To assemble the cups:** Place two pieces of the candied bacon and a pretzel rod in the back of each cup. Pour ¼ cup (35 g) of the smoked almonds into the base of each cup and place twelve to fifteen cheese crackers in and on top of the almonds.

7. Insert a peanut butter cup skewer in the middle back, a salami skewer in the right side, a pickle skewer in front of the salami skewer, and an everything bagel cheese truffle skewer in the middle.

8. Place two Gouda triangles, with points up, in the left side.

9. Garnish with a sprig of fresh rosemary.

FOURTH OF JULY FIREWORKS CUPS

These patriotic cups will go off with a bang! As kid friendly as they are adult friendly, these yummy cups can be enjoyed at an afternoon cookout or while watching fireworks later in the evening. Put them in recyclable cups for easy cleanup at the end of the night.

MAKES 6 CUPS

SUPPLIES

6 glasses or rigid plastic cups, 9 ounces (270 ml) in size

12 decorative picks, 4 inches (10 cm) long, divided

12 round skewers, 6 inches (15 cm) long

6 toothpicks, 4 inches (10 cm) long

2 mini star-shaped cookie cutters, one a little larger than the other

6 American flag picks (optional)

STRAWBERRY STAR SKEWERS

6 slices Havarti cheese (for cookie cutter)

3 large strawberries, trimmed and cut in half (for cookie cutter)

18 blueberries

MINI SWEET PEPPER SKEWERS

3 mini red sweet peppers, cut in half and seeded (for cookie cutter)

6 slices white cheddar cheese (for cookie cutter)

BABYBEL CHEESE SKEWERS

6 Babybel cheeses (for cookie cutter)

24 blueberries

TOMATO STAR SKEWERS

6 slices smoked Gouda cheese (for cookie cutter)

6 grape or cherry tomatoes

1. **To assemble the strawberry star skewers:** Cut out six star shapes each from the Havarti slices and the strawberry halves with the larger cookie cutter.

2. Thread six 4-inch (10 cm) decorative picks each with a Havarti star, a strawberry star, and 3 blueberries. Set aside.

3. **To assemble the mini sweet pepper skewers:** Cut out a star shape from each of the six mini pepper halves and six star shapes from the white cheddar slices with the smaller cookie cutter. Insert a mini white cheddar star into the star cutout of each mini red pepper half.

4. Holding the pointed ends up, thread six 6-inch (15 cm) round skewers each with a red pepper half, avoiding piercing through the top of the pepper. Set aside.

5. **To assemble the Babybel cheese skewers:** Cut out a star shape with the larger cookie cutter from the red wax of one side of each of the Babybel cheeses, exposing the white cheese inside.

6. Thread the remaining six 6-inch (15 cm) round skewers each with a blueberry, a Babybel cheese round with a star cutout, and three more blueberries. Set aside.

7. **To assemble the tomato star skewers:** Cut out six star shapes from the smoked Gouda slices with the larger cookie cutter.

8. Holding the pointed ends up, thread the six 4-inch (10 cm) toothpicks each with a cherry tomato and a smoked Gouda star, avoiding piercing through the top of the star. Set aside.

(continued)

SALAMI SKEWERS

18 slices salami, quarter-folded

ADDITIONAL INGREDIENTS

6 blue rock candy sticks

1½ cups (225 g) blueberries

12 to 18 star-shaped crackers (such as Valley Lahvosh brand)

6 red wrapped hard candies (optional)

 TIP JAR

Reserve the mini red pepper star-shaped cutouts in step 3 and cut out more star shapes with the smaller cookie cutter if there is any leftover space on the cheese slices. Add these stars to each of the cups.

9. **To assemble the salami skewers:** Thread the remaining six 4-inch (10 cm) decorative picks each with three quarter-folded slices of salami. Set aside.

10. **To assemble the cups:** Place a rock candy stick in the middle back of each cup, and then pour ¼ cup (38 g) of the blueberries into the base.

11. Insert the strawberry star skewer to the left of the rock candy stick and the mini sweet pepper skewer to the right of the candy. Then place the Babybel cheese skewer to the left of the strawberry star skewer, the salami skewer in the right side of the cup, and the tomato star skewer in front of the mini sweet pepper skewer.

12. Place two or three star-shaped crackers in the front of the cup, staggering them in height.

13. Place a piece of red-wrapped candy in the front (if using).

14. Decorate with an American flag pick (if using).

FOURTH OF JULY SPARKLER CONES

These simple yet visually appealing treats are guaranteed to burn bright at the holiday cookout! This is a fun project to involve the kids and have them help assemble the skewers.

MAKES 4 CONES

SUPPLIES

4 sugar cones

Mini star-shaped cookie cutter

12 round skewers, 6 inches (15 cm) long

SPARKLER SKEWERS

6 large strawberries, trimmed and cut in half (for cookie cutter)

48 blueberries

36 mini marshmallows

ADDITIONAL INGREDIENTS

8 tablespoons mixed diced strawberries and whole blueberries

4 teaspoons chocolate syrup (store-bought or see recipe on page 134)

🫙 TIP JAR

If you have extra time, dip the rims of the sugar cones in melted chocolate before assembling and let it harden. Don't worry about getting it perfect. The drips will look and taste delicious too!

1. **To assemble the sparkler skewers:** Cut out twelve star shapes from the strawberry halves with the cookie cutter.

2. Holding the pointed end up, thread each skewer with four blueberries and three mini marshmallows, alternating each ingredient. Top with a strawberry star. Set aside.

3. **To assemble the cones:** Set the cones upright in a holder to assemble. Fill each cone with 2 tablespoons of the mixed diced strawberries and blueberries.

4. Drizzle 1 teaspoon of the chocolate syrup on top of the fruit.

5. Insert three sparkler skewers into each cone.

HALLOWEEN SPOOKY SNACK CAULDRONS

Trick the kiddos into snacking on some savory and healthy treats before they head out to collect (and eat) all that candy!

MAKES 4 CAULDRONS

SUPPLIES

4 black containers or plastic cauldrons, 4 to 6 ounces (120 to 180 ml) in size

Mini B and O letter-shaped cookie cutters

12 decorative picks, 4 inches (10 cm) long

4 round skewers, 6 inches (15 cm) long

"BOO" SKEWERS

16 slices mild orange cheddar cheese (for cookie cutter)

MUMMY DOG SKEWERS

4 Mummy Dogs (see recipe on page 129)

PRETZEL GHOSTS

1 tube white cookie icing

8 small candy eyeballs

4 white chocolate–covered pretzels (such as Flipz brand)

ADDITIONAL INGREDIENTS

4 Witch Finger Pretzel Rods (see recipe on page 131)

1 cup (150 g) grapes

1 cup (150 g) blueberries

1. **To assemble the "BOO" skewers:** Cut out four letter Bs and eight letter Os from the orange cheddar slices with the cookie cutters.

2. Thread four decorative picks each with the letter B and thread eight decorative picks each with the letter O. Set aside.

3. **To assemble the mummy dog skewers:** Holding the pointed ends up, thread the four 6-inch (15 cm) skewers each with a Mummy Dog, avoiding piercing through the top. Set aside.

4. **To assemble the pretzel ghosts:** Place a small dot of white cookie icing onto the backs of two candy eyeballs and attach them to the areas right below the top holes of a yogurt-covered pretzel. Repeat for the remaining three pretzel ghosts. Set aside.

5. **To assemble the cauldrons:** Insert a mummy dog skewer in the back right of each cauldron and a Witch Finger Pretzel Rod in the back left.

6. Pour ¼ cup (38 g) of the grapes and ¼ cup (38 g) of the blueberries into the base of each cauldron, mixing them together a bit.

7. Insert a set of "BOO" letters in the back middle, varying their heights and placement.

8. Lay a pretzel ghost in front on top of the fruit, using the fruit to prop it up.

CHRISTMAS CHARCUTERIE CUPS

These cute appetizer cups are sure to bring some Christmas cheer! Combining the flavors of my Classic Jarcuterie (page 21) with some merry twists, they are perfect for entertaining at home during the holidays.

MAKES 6 CUPS

SUPPLIES

6 festive glasses, 4 ounces (120 ml) in size

6 loop or knotted flat skewers, 6 inches (15 cm) long

6 round skewers, 6 inches (15 cm) long

6 toothpicks, 4 inches (10 cm) long

Mini Christmas tree–shaped cookie cutter

SALAMI SKEWERS

6 pitted Castelvetrano olives

6 grape or cherry tomatoes

6 cubes Havarti cheese

6 slices salami, quarter-folded

CHRISTMAS TREE SKEWERS

6 slices dill Havarti cheese (for cookie cutter)

FRUIT SKEWERS

12 green grapes

6 raspberries

ADDITIONAL INGREDIENTS

6 pretzel rods

12 tablespoons pistachios without shells

6 rolled wafer cookies

6 strawberries, sliced ¾ inch (2 cm) from the base

12 sprigs fresh dill, for garnishing

1. **To assemble the salami skewers:** Thread the 6-inch (15 cm) loop skewers each with an olive, a tomato, a Havarti cube, and a quarter-folded slice of salami. Set aside.

2. **To assemble the Christmas tree skewers:** Cut out six Christmas tree shapes from the Havarti dill slices with the cookie cutter.

3. Holding the pointed ends up, thread the 6-inch (15 cm) round skewers each with a Havarti Christmas tree, avoiding piercing through the top of the tree. Set aside.

4. **To assemble the fruit skewers:** Holding the pointed ends up, thread the 4-inch (10 cm) toothpicks each with two grapes and a raspberry, avoiding piercing through the top of the raspberry. Set aside.

5. **To assemble the cups:** Place a pretzel rod in the back middle of each cup.

6. Pour 2 tablespoons of the pistachios into the base of each cup, and then place a rolled wafer cookie on top of the pistachios to the left of the pretzel.

7. Insert a salami skewer in the right side of each cup, a fruit skewer in the left side, and a Christmas tree skewer in the middle.

8. Place a strawberry on the front rim and garnish with two sprigs of fresh dill.

MINI CHRISTMAS TREE BOARDS

Deck your holiday table with edible mini Christmas trees! Of course, I absolutely love anything mini, but these trees top my list. Set these festive appetizers as place settings before serving Christmas dinner.

SUPPLIES

4 mini charcuterie boards, 3½ inches (9 cm) wide by 7½ inches (19 cm) long

2 mini star-shaped cookie cutters, one a little larger than the other

INGREDIENTS

16 slices white cheese, such as cheddar or Monterey Jack (for cookie cutter)

20 raspberries

8 pieces cheese straws (such as Mama Geraldine's brand), 2 inches (5 cm) long

12 grape tomatoes

8 cubes white cheese, such as cheddar, Monterey Jack, or pepper jack (for cookie cutter)

32 sprigs fresh rosemary, 3 inches (7.5 cm) long

12 dried cranberries

12 pretzel sticks

1. Cut out twelve smaller star shapes and four larger star shapes from the white cheese slices with the cookie cutters. Set aside.

2. **To assemble the mini boards:** Place five raspberries in an upside-down V shape at the bottom of each board.

3. Leave a small space above the raspberries and lay two cheese-straw pieces in an upside-down V shape.

4. Leave another small space above the cheese straws, and then lay three tomatoes, alternating with two cheese cubes, in an upside-down V shape.

5. Lay two sprigs of the rosemary in an upside-down V shape between each layer, starting with the space below the raspberries. (For this space, you may need shorter sprigs of rosemary.)

6. Place three smaller cheese stars across the raspberries and four dried cranberries across the cheese straws.

7. Top the tree with a larger star and place three pretzel sticks at the base for the trunk. (Break the pretzel sticks, if needed, to fit the space.)

NEW YEAR'S EVE COUPE GLASSES

Count down to midnight with good friends, nice bubbly, and these elegant coupe glasses! The adorable mini Brie clocks are a great reminder to keep track of time through all the merriment.

MAKES 6 COUPE GLASSES

SUPPLIES

6 coupe glasses

Edible ink pen

6 decorative picks, 4 inches (10 cm) long

CLOCK SKEWERS

6 mini Brie rounds, 0.9 ounce (25 g) in size

3 dried figs, cut in half

ADDITIONAL INGREDIENTS

12 tablespoons everything cashews or nuts of choice

6 bunches grapes of choice

12 star-shaped crackers (such as Valley Lahvosh brand)

6 slices prosciutto, folded into ribbons

6 dried apricots

1 green apple, cut into 12 to 18 thin slices

12 triangles aged Gouda cheese

6 chocolate truffles

12 waffle pretzels

6 sprigs fresh rosemary, for garnishing

1. **To assemble the clock skewers:** With the edible ink pen, draw a clockface with the hands pointing to midnight on each of the mini Brie rounds.

2. Thread the decorative picks each with a Brie clock and a fig half. Set aside.

3. **To assemble the coupe glasses:** Pour 2 tablespoons of the everything cashews in the back half of each glass and place a grape bunch in the front half, draping them over the front rim.

4. Place two star-shaped crackers in the back right of each glass and insert a clock skewer to the left of them.

5. Place two or three apple slices and a dried apricot in the right side.

6. Place a prosciutto ribbon in front of the Brie clock skewer and the Gouda triangles, with points up, in the front left.

7. Set a chocolate truffle and two waffle pretzels in the middle.

8. Garnish with a sprig of fresh rosemary.

SPECIAL OCCASIONS

Make any occasion a special occasion with jarcuterie! There are so many opportunities to turn an already-fun experience into something even more special. In this chapter, I share lots of ideas for enjoying get-togethers with friends and family, from celebrating birthdays to watching a movie or game at home to hosting brunch.

BIRTHDAY PARTY CANDY JARCUTERIE

This whimsical approach to jarcuterie is so sweet! There's nothing better than watching people's eyes light up when they see these colorful concoctions. The jars come together quickly, and you can customize them with your favorite sweets for party favors.

MAKES 4 JARS

SUPPLIES

4 glasses or jars, 7 to 8 ounces (210 to 240 ml) in size

4 decorative picks, 4 inches (10 cm) long

RAINBOW SKEWERS

4 rainbow sour candy belts

ADDITIONAL INGREDIENTS

3 cups (600 g) jelly beans, divided

4 Rainbow Sprinkle Pretzel Rods (see recipe on page 131)

4 rainbow-swirl lollipops

4 rock candy sticks

8 to 12 Strawberry Pocky

12 to 16 white chocolate–covered pretzels

24 to 28 Nerds Gummy Clusters

8 to 12 Sour Patch Kids

1. **To assemble the rainbow skewers:** Thread the decorative picks each with a rainbow sour candy belt in a wave pattern. Set aside.

2. **To assemble the jars:** Pour ½ cup (100 g) of the jelly beans into the base of each jar.

3. Insert a Rainbow Sprinkle Pretzel Rod, a lollipop, a rock candy stick, a rainbow belt skewer, and three or four Pocky in the back.

4. Add more jelly beans, about ¼ cup (50 g), then top with two or three chocolate-covered pretzels.

5. Fill in gaps with the Nerd Gummy Clusters and Sour Patch Kids.

MOVIE NIGHT POPCORN BOXES

Movie night is Certified Fresh™ with these popcorn boxes accented with colorful candies and cookies! I like to use classic movie snacks, but these boxes can be customized with family favorites, color schemes, or movie themes.

MAKES 6 POPCORN BOXES

SUPPLIES
6 popcorn boxes

54 round skewers, 6 inches (15 cm) long, divided

CANDY SKEWERS
24 Sour Patch Kids, divided

36 DOTS Gumdrops, divided

COOKIE SKEWERS
24 Oreo Minis, divided

12 white chocolate peanut butter cups

ADDITIONAL INGREDIENTS
12 to 14 cups (95 to 115 g) popped popcorn of choice

18 red licorice twists

6 tablespoons Milk Chocolate M&M's, with the brown ones removed

12 Pocky, flavors of choice

 TIP JAR

Not just for movie night, these popcorn boxes can be customized for birthdays or an event with a color scheme using colored popcorn.

1. **To assemble the candy skewers:** Holding the pointed ends up, thread eighteen skewers each with a Sour Patch Kid, avoiding piercing through the top of the gummy. Set aside.

2. Holding the pointed ends up, thread six skewers each with a DOTS Gumdrop, avoiding piercing through the top of the gumdrop. Set aside.

3. Holding the pointed ends up, thread six skewers each with three DOTS Gumdrops, avoiding piercing through the top gumdrop. Set aside.

4. Holding the pointed ends up, thread six skewers each with two DOTS Gumdrops and a Sour Patch Kid, avoiding piercing through the sour gummy. Set aside.

5. **To assemble the cookie skewers:** Holding the pointed ends up, thread twelve skewers each with an Oreo Mini, avoiding piercing through the top of the cookie. Set aside.

6. Holding the pointed ends up, thread the remaining six skewers each with a white chocolate peanut butter cup, an Oreo Mini, another peanut butter cup, and another Oreo, avoiding piercing through the top cookie. Set aside.

7. **To assemble the popcorn boxes:** Fill each popcorn box halfway full of popcorn. Place three red licorice twists in the back, varying their heights and using the popcorn to help hold them in place.

8. Add more popcorn to fill each box and sprinkle 1 tablespoon of M&M's on top.

9. Stick two Pocky in the back, anchoring them in the popcorn at varying heights.

10. Arrange the candy and cookie skewers however you like, anchoring them in the popcorn at various heights.

HAPPY HOUR SNACK MUGS

I love spending a happy hour with good friends, good beer, and good snacks! And that's what this one is all about. You'll love this combination of salty snacks that pair perfectly with an ice-cold beer at the end of a long day.

MAKES 6 MUGS

SUPPLIES

6 barrel-shaped wood mugs, 7 ounces (210 ml) in size

12 knotted flat skewers, 6 inches (15 cm) long, divided

MEAT AND CHEESE SKEWERS

12 cubes mild cheddar cheese

24 pieces meat sticks, ½ inch (1 cm) long, divided

12 cubes smoked cheddar cheese

6 cubes Colby Jack cheese

ADDITIONAL INGREDIENTS

6 pretzel rods

6 strips beef jerky

3 cups (180 g) bar snack mix (such as Utz Pub Mix), divided

1. **To assemble the meat and cheese skewers:** Thread six skewers each with a cheddar cube, a meat-stick piece, a smoked cheddar cube, another meat-stick piece, and a Colby Jack cube.

2. Thread the remaining six skewers each with a smoked cheddar cube, a meat-stick piece, a cheddar cube, and another meat-stick piece.

3. **To assemble the mugs:** Place a pretzel rod and a beef jerky strip in the back middle of each mug.

4. Fill each mug halfway full with the bar snack mix.

5. Insert one style of a meat and cheese skewer in the right side and the other style of a meat and cheese skewer in the left side.

6. Top each mug with the remaining bar snack mix.

GAME DAY APPETIZER CUPS

Think of your favorite essential game-day apps and these cups have you covered! They're especially great for guests who are busy watching the big game. You can hand these out while the game is on, or they can come grab one and get right back to it.

MAKES 6 CUPS

SUPPLIES

6 plastic cups, 4 ounces (120 ml) in size

6 loop or knotted flat skewers, 6 inches (15 cm) long

12 round skewers, 6 inches (15 cm) long, divided

6 decorative picks, 4 inches (10 cm) long

6 decorative flags (optional)

BUFFALO CHICKEN BITE SKEWERS

18 frozen buffalo chicken bites, cooked according to package directions

12 chunks blue cheese

BACON-WRAPPED MINI SAUSAGE SKEWERS

12 Bacon-Wrapped Mini Sausages (see recipe on page 128)

JALAPEÑO POPPER SKEWERS

6 frozen jalapeño poppers, cooked according to package directions

SMOKED ALMOND CHEESE TRUFFLE SKEWERS

12 Smoked Almond Cheese Truffles (see recipe on page 124)

ADDITIONAL INGREDIENTS

3 or 4 celery ribs

1½ cups (210 g) smoked almonds

18 everything bagel pretzel crisps

1. **To assemble the buffalo chicken bite skewers:** Thread the six 6-inch (15 cm) loop skewers each with three buffalo chicken bites and two blue cheese chunks, alternating the ingredients on the skewer. Set aside.

2. **To assemble the bacon-wrapped mini sausage skewers:** Thread six 6-inch (15 cm) round skewers each with two Bacon-Wrapped Mini Sausages. Set aside.

3. **To assemble the jalapeño popper skewers:** Thread the remaining six 6-inch (15 cm) round skewers each with a jalapeño popper. Set aside.

4. **To assemble the smoked almond cheese truffle skewers:** Thread the six 4-inch (10 cm) decorative picks each with two Smoked Almond Cheese Truffles. Set aside.

5. **To assemble the cups:** Cut the celery ribs into ½-inch-thick (6 mm) strips, and then cut those strips into four 6-inch-long (15 cm) sticks, four 5-inch-long (12.5 cm) sticks, and four 4-inch-long (10 cm) sticks for a total of eighteen celery sticks.

6. Place a 6-inch (15 cm), a 5-inch (12.5 cm), and a 4-inch (10 cm) celery stick in the back right of each cup, and then pour ¼ cup (35 g) of the smoked almonds into the base.

7. Insert a jalapeño popper skewer to the left of the celery sticks, a bacon-wrapped mini sausage skewer in the right side, and a buffalo chicken bite skewer in the left side.

8. Place a smoked almond cheese truffle skewer in the middle on top.

9. Decorate with a flag (if using) in the front of each cup.

HOME RUN SNACK BASKETS

Hit it out of the park with these kid-friendly baskets with all the essential baseball snacks! These are perfect for watching your favorite team or for a baseball-themed birthday party. Best of all, they are easy to put together and easy to clean up.

MAKES 6 BASKETS

SUPPLIES

6 plastic deli baskets

6 wax-paper liners

6 plastic condiment cups, 2 ounces (60 ml) in size

12 to 18 round skewers or lollipop sticks, 4 inches (10 cm) long

MINI CORN DOG SKEWERS

12 to 18 frozen mini corn dogs, cooked according to package directions

ADDITIONAL INGREDIENTS

1 bag sunflower seeds, 16 ounces (454 g) in size

1 bag peanuts in shells, 16 ounces (454 g) in size

6 boxes Cracker Jack, 1 ounce (28 g) in size

6 Baby Ruth Milk Chocolate Bars, Fun Size, wrapped

12 red licorice twists, tied into a knot

Ketchup and/or mustard, for topping the mini corn dogs

 TIP JAR

Instead of deli baskets, use baseball helmet ice cream bowls to hold all the fun snacks. You will need to downsize the ingredients for these smaller containers.

1. Line the deli baskets with the wax-paper liners and fill the condiment cups with the sunflower seeds. Set aside.

2. **To assemble the mini corn dog skewers:** Thread each skewer with a mini corn dog. Set aside.

3. **To assemble the baskets:** Fill each basket with peanuts and some of the Cracker Jack from each box.

4. Arrange a condiment cup of sunflower seeds, a Baby Ruth, two licorice knots, and two or three mini corn dog skewers in each basket. You can lay a Cracker Jack box with the leftovers in the basket or serve it on the side.

5. Top the mini corn dogs with the condiment of choice.

FRENCH TOAST BREAKFAST CUPS

Make breakfast extra special with these mini cups! Kids and adults alike will be delighted to dip the French toast sticks in the maple syrup at the bottom of the cup. With such a cute presentation and easy assembly and cleanup, you'll want to serve these on lots of occasions.

MAKES 6 CUPS

SUPPLIES

6 wood cups or jars, 4 ounces (120 ml) in size

#100 scoop or melon baller

6 round skewers, 6 inches (15 cm) long

FRUIT SKEWERS

½ cantaloupe

6 strawberries

24 to 36 blueberries

ADDITIONAL INGREDIENTS

6 tablespoons pure maple syrup

12 frozen French toast sticks, cooked according to package directions

12 Bacon Twists (see recipe on page 127)

6 sprigs fresh mint, for garnishing

 TIP JAR

I like to upcycle empty glass yogurt containers for these brunch cups, such as Yoplait Oui jars.

1. **To assemble the fruit skewers:** Scoop out six balls from the cantaloupe with the scoop or melon baller.

2. Thread each skewer with a strawberry, a cantaloupe ball, and four to six blueberries. Set aside.

3. **To assemble the cups:** Pour 1 tablespoon of the maple syrup into each cup.

4. Insert two French toast sticks in the right side of each cup, two bacon twists in the back middle, and a fruit skewer in the left side.

5. Garnish with a sprig of fresh mint.

BAGELS AND LOX BRUNCH CUPS

This unique and healthy take on bagels and lox is sure to become a brunch favorite! In these eye-catching cups, bagel chips replace traditional bagels, and the skewers have tasty bites of everything else: smoked salmon, cream cheese, capers, red onion, cucumber, and tomato.

MAKES 4 CUPS

SUPPLIES

4 glasses, 6 to 8 ounces (180 to 240 ml) in size

4 loop or knotted flat skewers, 6 inches (15 cm) long

4 loop or knotted flat skewers, 4 inches (15 cm) long

SMOKED SALMON ROLLS

2 packages sliced smoked salmon, 4 ounces (113 g) in size

DOUBLE CHEESE TRUFFLE SKEWERS

12 capers

4 Lemon Dill Cheese Truffles (see recipe on page 125)

8 rolls smoked salmon

4 pieces red onion, 1 inch (2.5 cm) in size

4 slices cucumber, cut with a wavy cutter

4 Everything Bagel Cheese Truffles (see recipe on page 124)

SINGLE CHEESE TRUFFLE SKEWERS

24 capers

4 grape or cherry tomatoes

8 rolls smoked salmon

4 Everything Bagel Cheese Truffles (see recipe on page 124)

4 slices cucumber, cut with a wavy cutter

4 pieces red onion, 1 inch (2.5 cm) in size

ADDITIONAL INGREDIENTS

1 cup (150 g) blueberries

8 to 12 bagel chips

4 sprigs fresh dill, for garnishing

4 thin wedges lemon, for garnishing

1. **To assemble the smoked salmon rolls:** Slice the smoked salmon into sixteen 1-inch (2.5 cm) strips, and then roll each strip from one end to the other. Set aside to use on the skewers.

2. **To assemble the double cheese truffle skewers:** Thread the 6-inch (15 cm) loop skewers each with three capers, a Lemon Dill Cheese Truffle, a salmon roll, an onion piece, a cucumber slice, another salmon roll, and an Everything Bagel Cheese Truffle. Set aside.

3. **To assemble the single cheese truffle skewers:** Thread the 4-inch (10 cm) loop skewers each with three capers, a tomato, a salmon roll, an Everything Bagel Cheese Truffle, another salmon roll, a cucumber slice, an onion piece, and three more capers. Set aside.

4. **To assemble the cups:** Pour ¼ cup (38 g) of the blueberries into the base of each cup.

5. Insert a double cheese truffle skewer in the right side and a single cheese truffle in the left side.

6. Place two or three bagel chips in the back middle of each cup.

7. Garnish with a sprig of fresh dill and a lemon slice on the front rim.

AROUND THE WORLD & SEASONAL

Jarcuterie can cover themes beyond specific occasions. I love to throw a happy hour or get-together that highlights a specific season or cuisine. It's a fun way to take an ordinary gathering to the next level. In this chapter, I'll show you a few of my favorites to get you started, and you can take it from there with your own ideas!

FIESTA JARCUTERIE

Cue the mariachi band because these eye-catching margarita glasses have fiesta written all over them! Serve these as appetizers or snacks for Cinco de Mayo or a Taco Tuesday happy hour get-together.

SUPPLIES
4 margarita glasses, 16 ounces (475 ml) in size
12 toothpicks, 4 inches (10 cm) long, divided
4 mini bottles Tajín
4 to 8 decorative flags (optional)

OLIVE SKEWERS
4 pitted Spanish olives
4 cubes mild cheddar cheese
4 grape or cherry tomatoes

FRUIT SKEWERS
4 cubes mango, cut 1 inch (2.5 cm) in size
4 cubes kiwi, cut 1 inch (2.5 cm) in size
4 cubes pineapple, cut 1 inch (2.5 cm) in size

CHEESE SKEWERS
4 cubes Colby Jack cheese
4 grape or cherry tomatoes
4 cubes pepper jack cheese

ADDITIONAL INGREDIENTS
8 tablespoons spicy peanuts, plus more for filling in gaps
12 triangle tortilla chips
4 frozen taquitos, cooked according to package directions
8 sticks jicama, cut ½ inch (1 cm) wide by 3 to 4 inches (7.5 to 10 cm) long
4 wedges cucumber
2 mini red sweet peppers, cut in half lengthwise and seeded
4 frozen mini tacos, cooked according to package directions
12 to 16 spicy rolled tortilla chips or sticks (such as Takis brand)
12 triangles Manchego cheese
8 sprigs fresh cilantro, for garnishing
4 wedges lime, for garnishing

1. **To assemble the olive skewers:** Thread four toothpicks each with an olive, a cheddar cube, and a tomato. Set aside.

2. **To assemble the fruit skewers:** Thread four toothpicks each with a mango, kiwi, and pineapple cube. Set aside.

3. **To assemble the cheese skewers:** Thread the remaining four toothpicks each with a Colby Jack cube, a tomato, and a pepper jack cube. Set aside.

4. **To assemble the margarita glasses:** Pour 2 tablespoons of the spicy peanuts into the base of each glass.

5. Add three tortilla chips in the middle back, and then lean a taquito in the middle against the tortilla chips.

6. Place two jicama sticks to the right of the taquito, with a cucumber wedge in front of it, and a mini pepper half to the left of the taquito.

7. Insert an olive skewer in the right side of each glass, a fruit skewer in the left side, and a cheese skewer in the middle.

8. Place a mini taco in the front right and a Tajín bottle in front of the mini pepper half.

9. Place 3 or 4 spicy rolled tortilla chips in front of the tortilla chips, and then fan three triangles of Manchego, with the points up, in the back left.

10. Fill in gaps with spicy peanuts, garnish with two sprigs of fresh cilantro, and place a lime wedge on the front rim.

11. Decorate with the flags (if using) in the sides of each glass.

 TIP JAR

Sprinkle the Tajín on the fruit skewers and jicama sticks for an extra punch of flavor. Save any leftover jicama to add to salads or a crudités platter.

GREEK LOADED HUMMUS RAMEKINS

Indulge in the fresh flavors of the Mediterranean! Not only delicious but also healthy, this loaded-hummus appetizer is sure to be a hit at any gathering.

MAKES 4 RAMEKINS

SUPPLIES
4 shallow ramekins, 4 ounces (120 ml) in size

INGREDIENTS
1 container hummus, 10 ounces (283 g) in size

12 baked pita chips (store-bought or see recipe on page 127)

4 baby carrots, cut in half lengthwise

8 slices cucumber, cut with a wavy cutter, plus 2 teaspoons diced cucumber, divided

4 mini sweet peppers, cut in half lengthwise and seeded

2 teaspoons crumbled feta cheese

2 teaspoons diced red onion

2 teaspoons diced green olives

2 teaspoons diced Kalamata olives

4 grape tomatoes, diced

1 tablespoon chopped fresh flat-leaf parsley, plus 4 sprigs for garnishing

8 tablespoons roasted chickpeas (store-bought or see recipe on page 126)

1. **To assemble the ramekins:** Spoon the hummus into each ramekin, dividing it evenly among them, about ⅓ cup (80 g) per ramekin.

2. Place three baked pita chips, with points up, in the left side of each ramekin.

3. Working left to right from the pita chips, place two carrot halves, two cucumber slices, and two mini pepper halves along the back of each ramekin.

4. Evenly sprinkle ½ teaspoon each of diced cucumber, crumbled feta, diced red onion, diced green olives, diced Kalamata olives, and diced tomatoes on the hummus in the front of each ramekin. Then, sprinkle some of the chopped parsley over the hummus toppings.

5. Place 2 tablespoons of the roasted chickpeas on the hummus between the cucumber slices and mini pepper halves.

6. Garnish with a sprig of fresh flat-leaf parsley.

ITALIAN JARCUTERIE

These gorgeous jars are filled with the flavors of Italy! Enjoy tortellini, caprese, Italian meats, and even a pipette filled with a balsamic glaze that perfectly complements every delicious bite.

SUPPLIES

6 jars, 8 ounces (240 ml) in size

6 plastic pipettes, 6 inches (15 cm) tall (3 ml capacity)

6 knotted flat skewers, 6 inches (15 cm) long

12 round skewers, 6 inches (15 cm) long, divided

BALSAMIC PIPETTES

¼ cup (60 ml) balsamic glaze

TORTELLINI SKEWERS

12 spinach tortellini, cooked according to package directions, drained, and patted dry with a paper towel

6 plain tortellini, cooked according to package directions, drained, and patted dry with a paper towel

CAPRESE SKEWERS

6 blackberries

18 bocconcini (mini mozzarella balls)

12 fresh basil leaves

12 grape or cherry tomatoes

SALAMI SKEWERS

6 pitted Castelvetrano olives

12 slices regular salami, quarter-folded

6 slices spicy salami, quarter-folded

6 pieces quartered marinated artichoke hearts

12 slices peppered salami

ADDITIONAL INGREDIENTS

1½ cups (150 g) Rosemary Olive Oil Walnuts (see recipe on page 130)

6 sesame grissini (breadsticks)

1. **To assemble the balsamic pipettes:** Pour the balsamic glaze into a glass. Remove the cap from a pipette (if it has one). Dip the pointy end of the pipette into the glaze in the glass and gently squeeze the top of the pipette to suck in the liquid. Fill to the desired amount. Wipe the pipette clean and replace the cap (if it has one). Repeat with the remaining five pipettes. Set aside.

2. **To assemble the tortellini skewers:** Thread the six knotted skewers each with a spinach tortellino, a plain tortellino, and another spinach tortellino. Set aside.

3. **To assemble the caprese skewers:** Thread six round skewers each with a blackberry, a bocconcino, a basil leaf, a tomato, another bocconcino, another basil leaf, and another tomato. Set aside.

4. **To assemble the salami skewers:** Thread the remaining six round skewers each with an olive, a quarter-folded slice of regular salami, a quarter-folded slice of spicy salami, a piece of artichoke heart, another quarter-folded slice of regular salami, and two slices of peppered salami. Set aside.

5. **To assemble the jars:** Pour ¼ cup (25 g) of the Rosemary Olive Oil Walnuts into the base of each jar. Place a sesame grissini in the back right.

6. Insert a tortellini skewer in the middle of each jar, a caprese skewer in the left side, and a salami skewer in the right side.

7. Place a peperoncino on the front rim of the jar. Insert a balsamic pipette in the back or front of the jar (wherever it fits best).

8. Insert two rosemary grissini in the back middle and left of the jar.

6 peperoncini, sliced ¾ inch (2 cm) from the base

12 rosemary grissini (breadsticks)

6 chunks Parmesan cheese, ¾ inch (2 cm) in size

6 sprigs fresh rosemary, for garnishing

9. Place a Parmesan chunk wherever you can fit it.

10. Garnish with a sprig of fresh rosemary.

ASIAN-INSPIRED APPETIZER CUPS

These eye-catching appetizer cups make for a flavorful start to an Asian meal! They're also a great excuse to visit a local Asian market and discover new snacks and foods.

MAKES 4 CUPS

SUPPLIES

4 glasses, 6 to 8 ounces (180 to 240 ml) in size

Mini flower-shaped cookie cutter

8 toothpicks, 4 inches (10 cm) long, divided

4 round skewers, 6 inches (15 cm) long

PAPAYA FLOWER SKEWERS

1 papaya, seeded and sliced ½ inch (1 cm) thick (for cookie cutter)

EVERYTHING BAGEL CHEESE TRUFFLE SKEWERS

8 Everything Bagel Cheese Truffles (see recipe on page 124)

COCONUT SHRIMP SKEWERS

4 frozen coconut shrimp, cooked according to package directions

ADDITIONAL INGREDIENTS

1 cup (90 g) wasabi peas, plus more for filling in gaps

8 to 12 Wonton Crackers (see recipe on page 126)

4 wasabi-flavored roasted seaweed snack sheets

12 Matcha Green Tea Pocky

20 edamame pods, steamed

1. **To assemble the papaya flower skewers:** Cut twelve flower shapes out of the papaya slices with the cookie cutter.

2. Holding the pointed ends up, thread four 4-inch (10 cm) toothpicks each with three papaya flowers, avoiding piercing through the top flower. Set aside.

3. **To assemble the everything bagel cheese truffle skewers:** Thread the remaining four 4-inch (10 cm) toothpicks each with two Everything Bagel Cheese Truffles. Set aside.

4. **To assemble the coconut shrimp skewers:** Thread the four 6-inch (15 cm) round skewers each with a coconut shrimp.

5. **To assemble the cups:** Pour ¼ cup (23 g) of the wasabi peas into the base of each glass.

6. Insert a coconut shrimp skewer in the back right, and then place two or three Wonton Crackers to the left of the coconut shrimp, varying them in height.

7. Insert a papaya flower skewer in front of the crackers and an everything bagel cheese truffle skewer in the front of each jar.

8. Slip a roasted seaweed sheet in the back left behind the crackers, allowing the other items to hold it in place.

9. Space out three Pocky in the back of the glass.

10. Fill in gaps with five edamame pods and more wasabi peas.

SPRING FLOWERPOTS

Welcome spring with these mini flowerpots blooming with beautiful foods! They are fun and fresh way to present healthy snacks for kids and adults at any kind of spring gathering.

MAKES 4 FLOWERPOTS

SUPPLIES

4 mini plastic flowerpots, 6 ounces (180 ml) in size

4 round skewers, 6 inches (15 cm) long

8 round skewers, 5 inches (12.5 cm) long

24 round skewers, 4 inches (10 cm) long, divided

Butterfly-shaped cookie cutters, about 2½ (5 cm) inches (6.5 cm) in size

Variety of mini flower-shaped cookie cutters

CATERPILLAR SKEWERS

4 red grapes

12 green grapes

8 small candy eyes

1 tube white cookie icing

BUTTERFLY SKEWERS

1 small watermelon, sliced ½ inch (1 cm) thick (for cookie cutter)

1 small cantaloupe, seeded and sliced ½ inch (1 cm) thick (for cookie cutter)

FLOWER SKEWERS

2 large strawberries, trimmed and cut in half (for cookie cutter)

1 large cucumber, sliced ½ inch (1 cm) thick (for cookie cutter)

6 slices cheese, such as mild orange and white cheddar, dill Havarti, Havarti, and Colby Jack (for cookie cutter)

2 radishes, cut in half and shaped into 4 tulips

48 leaves fresh basil (see Tip Jar below)

ADDITIONAL INGREDIENTS

1 cup (150 g) grapes

1 cup (60 g) pretzel balls

4 gummy worms

1. **To assemble the caterpillar skewers:** Holding the pointed ends up, thread the four 6-inch (15 cm) skewers each with a red grape and three green grapes, avoiding piercing through the top of the red grape. Glue two candy eyes on each red grape using the white cookie icing. Set aside.

2. **To assemble the butterfly skewers:** Cut out four butterflies each from the watermelon and cantaloupe for a total of eight butterflies. Holding the pointed ends up, thread the eight 5-inch (12.5 cm) skewers each with a butterfly, avoiding piercing through the top of the butterfly. Set aside.

3. **To assemble the flower skewers:** Cut out four flowers each from the strawberries and cucumber and twelve flowers from the cheese slices for a total of twenty flowers.

4. Holding the pointed ends up, thread twenty 4-inch (10 cm) skewers each with two basil leaves, 1 inch (2.5 cm) down from the top point. Top each skewer with a strawberry, cucumber, or cheese flower, avoiding piercing through the top of the flower. Set aside.

5. Holding the pointed ends up, thread the remaining four 4-inch (10 cm) skewers each with two basil leaves, 1 inch (2.5 cm) down from the top point, and a radish tulip, avoiding piercing through the top of the tulip. Set aside.

6. **To assemble the flowerpots:** Pour ¼ cup (38 g) of the grapes into the base of each flowerpot, and then top with ¼ cup (30 g) of the pretzel balls. Place a gummy worm hanging over the edge of the pot, and then insert a caterpillar skewer in the back right.

7. Insert the flower and butterfly skewers around the flowerpot, varying the heights. Insert the radish tulip in the front.

 TIP JAR

To give your flower skewers leaves, fold the ends of two basil leaves in half and slightly overlap the folded parts when placing them on a skewer in step 6.

SUMMER CLIP-ON SNACK CONES

Make a splash with these adorable clip-on cones! I love serving the kids these quick and easy mini cones at a pool party or when friends are over to swim. Accompanied by a refreshing drink, they are just the right size for a swim snack break.

MAKES 6 MINI CONES

SUPPLIES

6 glasses, size of choice

6 disposable mini wood cones, 5.1 inches (13 cm) tall

6 mini clothespins

6 drink umbrellas

6 paper straws

INGREDIENTS

Ice cubes

Blue drink of choice

6 meat sticks, cut 4½ inches (11.5 cm) long

1½ cups (80 g) Goldfish Crackers

6 Teddy Grahams Chocolate Graham Snacks

6 peach gummy rings

1. Clip a cone to each glass with a clothespin (see Tip Jar below).

2. **To assemble the clip-on cones:** Place a meat stick in the back right of each cone.

3. Pour ¼ cup (13 g) of the Goldfish Crackers into the base of each cone.

4. Place a Teddy Graham inside a peach gummy ring and set it on top of the crackers.

5. Stick a drink umbrella into each cone and add a paper straw to each glass.

 TIP JAR

You can pour the drink into the glasses before or after you assemble the cones. In order to prevent the glasses from tipping over while assembling the cones, adding the drink first will give the glasses some weight.

SWEET & SALTY FALL SNACK JARS

There's so much to love about fall, including these snack jars! They are perfect for an after-school treat or a fall event, or package them up in plastic party-favor bags and tie closed with a cute fall ribbon for some special deliveries.

MAKES 4 JARS

SUPPLIES
4 glasses or jars, 8 ounces (240 ml) in size
4 round skewers, 6 inches (15 cm) long
4 round skewers, 5 inches (12.5 cm) long

CARAMEL APPLE POPS
1 apple, cut into 8 wedges
1 container caramel dip, 16 ounces (454 g) in size
⅓ cup (35 g) chopped peanuts

ADDITIONAL INGREDIENTS
4 Fall Foliage Pretzel Rods (see recipe on page 132)
2 cups (120 g) snack mix (such as Chex Mix)
8 gingersnap cookies, divided
8 pieces Fall Bark (see recipe on page 132)

 TIP JAR

Toffee bits or mini chocolate chips are also great toppings for the caramel apple pops.

1. **To assemble the caramel apple pops:** Holding the pointed ends up, thread the 6-inch (15 cm) and 5-inch (12.5 cm) skewers each with an apple wedge, avoiding piercing through the top of the apple.

2. Dip each apple wedge in the caramel dip, and then coat with the chopped peanuts. Set aside.

3. **To assemble the glasses:** Place a Fall Foliage Pretzel Rod in the back right of each glass, and then pour ½ cup (30 g) of the snack mix into the base.

4. Place a gingersnap in the back left, and then insert a 6-inch (15 cm) and a 5-inch caramel apple pop in the back to the left of the pretzel rod. Place another gingersnap in front of the caramel apple pops. The gingersnaps will help hold the caramel apple pops in place.

5. Place two pieces of the Fall Bark in the front.

WINTER HOT CHOCOLATE CUPS

After the kids spend the day playing in the snow, warm them up with these cute and cozy cups! They are chock-full of toppings and dippers to go with a steaming mug of hot chocolate.

MAKES 6 JARS

SUPPLIES
4 jars, 4 ounces (120 ml) in size
4 round skewers, 4 inches (10 cm) long

POLAR BEAR SKEWERS
6 Polar Bear Cookies (see recipe on page 133)

ADDITIONAL INGREDIENTS
6 Yeti Pretzel Rods (see recipe on page 133)

1½ cups (75 g) mini marshmallows

6 Biscoff cookies

12 Cookies & Cream Pocky

6 tablespoons Junior Mints

6 tablespoons mini dark chocolate nonpareils (such as Sno-Caps candy)

Blue, silver, and white sprinkle mixture, for garnishing

1. **To assemble the polar bear skewers:** Holding the pointed end up, thread each skewer into the base of a Polar Bear Cookie, avoiding piercing through the top of the cookie. Set aside.

2. **To assemble the jars:** Place a Yeti Pretzel Rod in the back middle of each jar, and then pour ¼ cup (19 g) of the mini marshmallows into the base.

3. Place a Biscoff cookie in the right side with two Pocky behind it.

4. Insert a polar bear skewer in the left side.

5. Top the mini marshmallows in the front with 1 tablespoon each of the Junior Mints and the nonpareils.

6. Garnish with the sprinkles.

JUST FOR FUN

Think outside the jar with the ideas included in this chapter. You don't need to have a special occasion! Some of these are great for teacher appreciation, housewarming gifts, or just because.

RAINBOW BOXES

These rainbow boxes are a feast for the eyes and fun to assemble with the kids! Make them for birthday parties, Saint Patrick's Day, or a special after-school snack when friends come over. There are no set rules on this one—I like to use a mix of savory and sweet items and have made some suggestions below.

MAKES 4 BOXES

SUPPLIES

4 shallow white boxes with clear lids, about 3 inches (7.5 cm) wide by 7 (18 cm) inches long

4 lengths white ribbon (optional)

4 rainbow-swirled lollipops (optional)

SUGGESTED INGREDIENTS

Red foods: Strawberries, raspberries, apple slices, cherry or grape tomatoes, mini sweet peppers, pepperoni slices, fruit leather, jelly beans, cherry sours, Swedish fish, gummy candies, licorice

Orange foods: Orange slices, dried mango, dried apricot, baby carrots, Goldfish Crackers, cheddar cheese cubes, jelly beans, gummy candies

Yellow foods: Cherry or grape tomatoes, mini sweet peppers, banana chips, dried plaintains, dried pineapple, jelly beans, lemon sours, gummy candies

Green foods: Grapes, apple slices, pea crisps, pistachios without shells, jelly beans, gummy candies, sour apple licorice

Blue foods: Blueberries, Concord grapes, jelly beans, gummy candies, blue raspberry licorice

Purple foods: Blackberries, red grapes, wine-soaked cheese (for adults), jelly beans, gummy candies

1. **To assemble the boxes:** Arrange the ingredients in even sections, from left to right, in the order of the colors of a rainbow: red, orange, yellow, green, blue, and purple.

2. Fit the lid on each box, and then decorate each box with a length of white ribbon (if using) tied into a bow, securing a lollipop (if using) in the bow.

BARKUTERIE PUP CUPS

Why would I make cups just for dogs? Because pets are people too! Well, they are at my house at least. We love celebrating our dog, and barkuterie is a clever way to do it. We also enjoy when friends bring their dogs over for a playdate and we can send them home with a cup full of treats.

MAKES 2 CUPS

SUPPLIES

2 disposable slanted wood cups, 6 ounces (170 g) in size

INGREDIENTS

4 bacon-style dog treats

2 green dental dog treats

2 rawhide-stuffed twists

⅔ cup (80 g) dry dog food

4 mini hot dog–shaped dog treats

4 fun-size bacon-style dog treats

4 to 16 mini bone-shaped dog treats (depending on the size of the bones)

2 T-bone-steak dog treats

1. **To assemble the cups:** From left to right in the back of each cup, place a bacon strip, a dental treat, another bacon strip, and a rawhide-stuffed twist.

2. Pour ⅓ cup (40 g) of the dog food into the base of each cup, and then place a hot-dog treat in the right side, two fun-size bacon treats in front of the hot dog, and another hot dog in the front middle.

3. Place the mini dog bones in the front left of each cup.

4. Top the middle of each cup with a T-bone-steak treat.

S'MORES KITS

We love to entertain, and one of the simplest and tastiest ways to wrap up an evening with friends is to gather around the firepit and make s'mores! Everyone gets their own kit, so there's no worry about everyone touching everything, things spilling or getting knocked over, and bugs getting into the food.

MAKES 4 KITS

SUPPLIES
4 clear stand-up pouch bags

INGREDIENTS
16 graham crackers

4 Hershey's Milk Chocolate Candy Bars, unwrapped

24 to 32 regular-size marshmallows

4 peanut butter cups, unwrapped

4 Ghirardelli Milk Chocolate Caramel Squares

 TIP JAR

Customize these with your favorite s'mores toppings like different chocolate candies or single-serve portions of peanut butter or hazelnut spread.

1. **To assemble each kit:** Place four graham crackers in the right side of each bag and a Hershey's bar in the back.

2. Drop six to eight marshmallows in front of the chocolate bar.

3. Place a peanut butter cup and caramel square in front of the marshmallows.

FARMERS MARKET GIFT BASKETS

Nothing compares to farm-to-table freshness! Show your support for your friends (and local farmers and purveyors) with these personalized baskets that are ideal gifts for hosts, teachers, housewarmings, and get well wishes. You can easily substitute ingredients with what's in season.

MAKES 4 BASKETS

SUPPLIES

4 pulp berry baskets, 1 pint (16 ounces, or 475 ml) in size

4 mini jelly jars with lids, 1.5 to 2 ounces (45 to 60 ml) in size

4 mini wood honey dippers

4 mini wood spreaders

MINI HONEY JARS

6 to 8 ounces (170 to 225 g) local honey

ADDITIONAL INGREDIENTS

4 small loaves artisan bread (or brioche rolls that look like small loaves)

4 Herb-Marinated Goat Cheese Mini Jars (see recipe on page 130)

24 to 30 strawberries

24 to 30 blackberries

 TIP JAR

While you're at the farmers market, look for some flowering herbs or food-safe flowers to embellish the baskets with.

1. **To assemble the mini honey jars:** Fill the four mini jelly jars each with local honey and fasten the lids. Set aside.

2. **To assemble the baskets:** Nestle a small loaf of bread in the back-left corner of each basket.

3. Prop a mini honey jar in the back-right corner and an Herb-Marinated Goat Cheese Mini Jar in the front-right corner.

4. Fill in the spaces around the bread and jars with the strawberries and blackberries.

5. Place a mini honey dipper and a mini spreader on top.

SNACKLE BOX

This box is such a cute play on a tackle box. It's also a convenient way to pack snacks for a fishing trip, a day at the lake, an outing at the park, or a road trip!

MAKES 1 BOX

SUPPLIES

1 brand-new plastic organizer box with a lid, washed and dried

SUGGESTED INGREDIENTS

Sausage snack bites

Spicy peanuts

Corn nuts

Braided pretzels

Mini chocolate chip cookies

Swedish Fish Tails

Mini Tropical Swedish Fish

Peach gummy rings

Small bunch grapes

Gummy worms

1. **To assemble the box:** Fill each of the compartments with the ingredients, using just enough to fill each compartment.

2. Hide a gummy worm or two within the ingredients for a surprise.

 TIP JAR

Your box may vary in size and compartments, but you can easily adjust everything to accommodate it.

PENCIL SNACK BOX

Score an A-plus when you surprise your star student with this adorable pencil box turned snack box! Pack this pencil box full of surprises for a back-to-school, an after-school, or a study-break snack.

MAKES 1 BOX

SUPPLIES

1 brand-new pencil box with a lid, washed and dried

5 or 6 toothpicks, 3 to 4 inches (7.5 to 10 cm) long (depending on the width of the pencil box), divided

1 brand-new pencil sharpener, washed and dried

1 edible ink pen

MINI PENCIL SKEWERS

1 thick cheddar cheese stick

1 mozzarella cheese stick, cut into three ¾-inch (2 cm) sections

1 meat stick, cut into ¼- to ½-inch (0.6 to 1 cm) sections (depending on the proportions of the mini pencils)

TURKEY SKEWERS

1 thick slice deli turkey, cut into 4 or 6 strips ¾ inch (2 cm) wide (cut 6 strips for a larger box and 4 for a smaller box)

ADDITIONAL INGREDIENTS

4 mini toasts

1 Rockit miniature apple

3 mini chocolate chip cookies

20 Goldfish Crackers

1 small bunch grapes

1 strawberry, cut in half lengthwise

1. **To assemble the mini pencil skewers:** Stand the cheddar cheese stick upright, and using a knife, slice each corner from top to bottom, shaving off a small sliver, to make it an octagon shape. Cut the cheese stick into three equal-size pieces for the bodies of the pencils. Set aside.

2. Shave off pieces from the three mozzarella sections to create the pencil tips. The wide parts of the tips should be the same width as the cheddar pencil bodies. Use the edible ink pen to color in the pointed ends to look like lead. Place the mozzarella shavings into the pencil sharpener. Set the tips and pencil sharpener aside.

3. Holding the pointed ends up, thread three toothpicks each with a meat-stick piece (for the eraser), a cheddar pencil body, and a mozzarella pencil tip, avoiding piercing through the top of the pencil tip. Set aside. (You may need to adjust the lengths of the parts of your pencils depending on the width of the pencil box; you want the pencils to be about three-quarters of the box's width.)

4. **To assemble the turkey skewers:** Thread the remaining two or three toothpicks each with two strips of turkey stacked together in a wave pattern. Set aside.

5. **To assemble the pencil boxes:** Place the pencil sharpener in the top-right corner and the four mini toasts below it.

6. Place the apple in the top-left corner and the three chocolate chip cookies below it.

7. Lay the three mini pencil skewers to the left of the pencil sharpener and the two or three turkey skewers to the right of the apple.

8. Fill in the space below the mini pencil skewers with the Goldfish Crackers and the space below the turkey skewers with the grapes, blueberries, and strawberry halves.

9. Fill in any gaps with more grapes and blueberries.

PICNIC SANDWICH PACKS

Everyone loves a picnic, and these portable packs make it easy to picnic anywhere! Enjoy them at the park, the lake, or even in your own backyard. You can customize them with your favorite sandwich fixings or go with the classic turkey and ham sandwich options here.

MAKES 2 BOXES

SUPPLIES

2 bakery boxes, 6 x 6 inches (15 x 15 cm) in size

4 round skewers, 6 inches (15 cm) long, divided

TURKEY SANDWICH SKEWERS

2 pitted black olives

1 slice bread, cut into 6 pieces

Mayonnaise, to taste

1 slice extra-sharp cheddar cheese, cut into quarters

2 slices turkey, cut in half and folded or rolled

1 slice cooked bacon, cut into 4 pieces

4 pieces leaf lettuce, folded or rolled

4 grape or cherry tomatoes

HAM SANDWICH SKEWERS

2 petite dill pickles, patted dry with a paper towel

1 slice bread, cut into 6 pieces

Dijon mustard, to taste

1 slice Swiss cheese, cut into quarters

2 slices ham, cut in half and folded or rolled

4 pieces leaf lettuce, folded or rolled

4 grape or cherry tomatoes

ADDITIONAL INGREDIENTS

1 bag sweet-potato chips, 6 to 8 ounces (170 to 225 g) in size

8 small pieces dark chocolate

2 small bunches grapes

16 to 20 blueberries

1. **To assemble the turkey sandwich skewers:** Thread two skewers each with an olive, a piece of bread with mayonnaise on it, a cheddar cheese quarter, a turkey slice, a bacon piece, a lettuce piece, and a tomato. Repeat with another piece of bread with mayonnaise and the remaining cheese, turkey, bacon, lettuce, and tomato, followed by a third piece of bread with mayonnaise. Set aside.

2. **To assemble the ham sandwich skewers:** Thread the remaining two skewers each with a pickle, a piece of bread with Dijon on it, a Swiss cheese quarter, a ham slice, a lettuce piece, and a tomato. Repeat with another piece of bread with Dijon and the remaining cheese, ham, lettuce, and tomato, followed by a third piece of bread with Dijon. Set aside.

3. **To assemble the boxes:** Lay a turkey sandwich skewer and a ham sandwich skewer diagonally in the box.

4. Fill in the area around the tops of the sandwich skewers with sweet-potato chips.

5. Fill in gaps below the sandwich skewers with the blueberries and grapes. Place four pieces of the dark chocolate in the bottom-right corner.

 TIP JAR

Feel free to explore more gourmet sandwich combinations, like ham, apple, and brie, or vegetarian options, like pesto, tomatoes, and mozzarella. Also, use different types of bread. The possibilities are endless!

RECIPES

can't emphasize enough how flexible jarcuterie can be. You can use all store-bought items or add a homemade touch, like I did with these recipes found throughout the projects in this book. Anything goes!

EVERYTHING BAGEL CHEESE TRUFFLES

MAKES ABOUT 25 TRUFFLES

8 ounces (227 g) cream cheese, softened

Everything bagel seasoning, to taste

1. Use a #100 scoop to scoop the cream cheese into balls. You can leave them domed with a flat side, like the shape of the scoop, or you can roll them into balls with your hands.

2. Roll the cheese balls in the everything bagel seasoning to coat.

SMOKED ALMOND CHEESE TRUFFLES

MAKES 30 TO 35 TRUFFLES

8 ounces (227 g) cream cheese, softened

1 cup (90 g) shredded extra-sharp cheddar cheese

½ teaspoon garlic powder

¼ teaspoon onion powder

Chopped smoked almonds, to taste

1. In a medium bowl, mix together the cream cheese, cheddar cheese, garlic powder, and onion powder.

2. Use a #100 scoop to scoop the cream cheese mixture into balls. You can leave them domed with a flat side, like the shape of the scoop, or you can roll them into balls with your hands.

3. Roll the cheese balls in the chopped smoked almonds to coat.

FLORAL CHEESE TRUFFLES

MAKES ABOUT 25 TRUFFLES

4 ounces (113 g) honey goat cheese

4 ounces (113 g) cream cheese

Dried edible flowers (such as lavender, calendula, rose), to taste

1. In a medium bowl, mix together the goat cheese and cream cheese.

2. Use a #100 scoop to scoop the cheese mixture into balls. You can leave them domed with a flat side, like the shape of the scoop, or you can roll them into balls with your hands.

3. Roll the cheese balls in the dried flowers to coat.

LEMON DILL CHEESE TRUFFLES

MAKES ABOUT 25 TRUFFLES

4 ounces (113 g) goat cheese

4 ounces (113 g) cream cheese

½ teaspoon garlic powder

4 to 5 tablespoons chopped fresh dill

Zest of 1 lemon

1. In a medium bowl, mix together the goat cheese, cream cheese, and garlic powder.

2. Use a #100 scoop to scoop the cheese mixture into balls. You can leave them domed with a flat side, like the shape of the scoop, or you can roll them into balls with your hands.

3. In a small bowl, combine the fresh dill and lemon zest.

4. Roll the cheese balls in the lemon-dill mixture to coat.

ROASTED CHICKPEAS

MAKES ABOUT 1½ CUPS (300 G)

1 can chickpeas, 15 to 15.5 ounces (425 to 439 g) in size
¼ teaspoon cumin
½ teaspoon garlic powder
½ teaspoon onion powder
½ teaspoon paprika
½ teaspoon salt
2 tablespoons olive oil

1. Preheat the oven to 425°F (220°C; gas mark 7). Line a baking sheet with parchment paper and set aside.

2. Drain the chickpeas, pat dry with a towel, and discard any loose skins. Transfer the chickpeas to the prepared baking sheet, arranging them in a single layer.

3. In a small bowl, mix together the cumin, garlic powder, onion powder, paprika, and salt.

4. Pour the olive oil over the chickpeas and toss to coat.

5. Sprinkle the seasoning mix over the chickpeas and toss to coat.

6. Bake for about 25 minutes, shaking the pan halfway through the baking time, or until crisp. Depending on the chickpeas and the humidity in your area, it could take a little longer for the chickpeas to get crispy.

7. Let cool before serving.

WONTON CRACKERS

MAKES 12 WONTON CRACKERS

4 square or rectangular wonton wrappers
Vegetable oil
Everything bagel seasoning, to taste

1. Preheat the oven to 375°F (190°C; gas mark 5). Line a baking sheet with parchment paper and set aside.

2. Lay out the wonton wrappers and cut each one into three strips. Transfer the wonton strips to the prepared baking sheet, arranging them in a single layer.

3. Brush the wonton strips with vegetable oil, and then evenly sprinkle with everything bagel seasoning. Press the seasoning into the wonton wrappers to help it stick.

4. Bake for about 5 minutes, or until crisp.

5. Let cool before serving.

BAKED PITA CHIPS

MAKES 24 PITA CHIPS

2 or 3 pita breads

Olive oil

Oregano, to taste

Salt, to taste

1. Preheat the oven to 375°F (190°C; gas mark 5). Line a baking sheet with parchment paper and set aside.

2. Cut the pitas in half, and then cut each half into four or six triangles. Transfer the triangles to the prepared baking sheet, arranging them in a single layer.

3. Brush the triangles with olive oil, and then evenly sprinkle with oregano and salt.

4. Bake for about 10 minutes, or until crisp, turning the pita chips over halfway through the baking time.

5. Let cool before serving.

BACON TWISTS

MAKES 16 TO 20 BACON TWISTS

1 package bacon, 16 ounces (454 g) in size (16 to 20 slices)

¼ cup (45 g) brown sugar

1. Preheat the oven to 350°F (175°C; gas mark 4). Line a baking sheet with aluminum foil.

2. Arrange the bacon slices in a single layer on the prepared baking sheet, and then sprinkle about ½ teaspoon of brown sugar onto each slice.

3. Spread and pat the brown sugar onto the bacon slices with your fingers or the back of a spoon.

4. Tightly twist each slice of bacon.

5. Bake for about 25 minutes, or until crisp, turning the twists over halfway through the baking time.

6. Remove from the pan and let cool before serving.

CANDIED BACON STRIPS

MAKES 16 TO 20 BACON STRIPS

1 package bacon, 16 ounces (454 g) in size (16 to 20 slices)

¼ cup (45 g) brown sugar

1. Preheat the oven to 350°F (175°C; gas mark 4). Line a baking sheet with aluminum foil.

2. Arrange the bacon slices on the prepared baking sheet in a single layer, and then sprinkle about ½ teaspoon of brown sugar onto each slice.

3. Spread and pat the brown sugar onto the bacon slices with your fingers or the back of a spoon.

4. Bake for 25 to 30 minutes, turning the strips over halfway through the baking time, until crisp.

5. Remove from the pan and let cool before serving.

BACON-WRAPPED MINI SAUSAGES

MAKES ABOUT 35 WRAPPED SAUSAGES

1 package bacon, 16 ounces (454 g) in size (16 to 20 slices)

1 package mini smoked sausages (such as Hillshire Farm Lit'l Smokies), 12 ounces (340 g) in size

32 to 40 toothpicks, 3 inches (7.5 cm) in size

½ cup (90 g) brown sugar

1. Preheat the oven to 325°F (160°C; gas mark 3). Line a baking sheet with parchment paper and set aside.

2. Cut the bacon slices in half.

3. Wrap a half slice of bacon around a mini smoked sausage, and then secure with a toothpick. Set aside. Repeat until you run out of bacon, smoked sausages, or both.

4. Add the brown sugar and wrapped sausages to a 1-gallon resealable plastic bag or container. Shake to coat thoroughly. Transfer the coated wrapped sausages to the prepared baking sheet, arranging them in a single layer.

5. Bake for about 40 minutes, or until the bacon is crisp.

6. Let cool and remove toothpicks, if desired, before serving.

MUMMY DOGS

MAKES ABOUT 35 MUMMY DOGS

1 package refrigerated crescent roll dough, 8 ounces (226 g) in size

1 package mini smoked sausages (such as Hillshire Farm Lit'l Smokies), 12 ounces (340 g) in size

Mustard and/or ketchup

1 toothpick

1. Preheat the oven to 375°F (190°C; gas mark 5). Line a baking sheet with parchment paper and set aside.

2. Unroll the crescent dough onto a piece of parchment paper, and then press it together at the perforations.

3. Cut the dough into ¼-inch-thick (6 mm) strips.

4. Wrap each sausage with enough dough to cover the entire sausage, leaving a small area for a face. Set onto the prepared baking sheet. Repeat with the remaining sausages and dough strips.

5. Bake for 12 to 14 minutes, until golden brown.

6. Let cool, and then add mustard and/or ketchup dots for eyes using the toothpick.

CUCUMBER CANAPÉS

MAKES 20 CANAPÉS

4 ounces (113 g) whipped cream cheese

1 tablespoon mayonnaise

1 teaspoon chopped fresh dill

1 teaspoon chopped fresh chives

Salt, to taste

Fresh cracked black pepper, to taste

10 slices white bread, crusts trimmed off and cut in half diagonally

1 to 2 English cucumbers

1. In a medium bowl, mix together the cream cheese, mayonnaise, dill, chives, salt, and pepper. Set aside.

2. Lay out the bread triangles and coat one side of each triangle with the cream cheese mixture.

3. Cut the ends off the cucumber(s) and stand it upright on a cutting board. Remove the peel on two sides by thinly slicing it off and then discarding. Cut the remaining cucumber into thin slices lengthwise. Set aside.

4. Top each bread triangle with three overlapping slices of cucumber. Carefully turn each triangle over on the cutting board so that the cucumber side is facedown and trim the length of the cucumber slices so that they are even with the edge of the bread.

ROSEMARY OLIVE OIL WALNUTS

MAKES 1½ CUPS (175 G)

1½ cups (175 g) walnuts

1 tablespoon extra-virgin olive oil

1½ teaspoons finely chopped fresh rosemary

Salt, to taste

1. Stir together the walnuts, olive oil, and rosemary in a medium skillet.

2. Heat over medium heat for 5 to 10 minutes, until toasted and fragrant.

3. Remove from the heat and sprinkle with salt.

4. Let cool before serving.

HERB-MARINATED GOAT CHEESE MINI JARS

MAKES 4 MINI JARS

4 mini jelly jars with lids, 1.5 to 2 ounces (45 to 60 ml) in size

½ teaspoon chopped fresh basil

½ teaspoon chopped fresh rosemary

½ teaspoon chopped fresh thyme

½ teaspoon chopped fresh oregano

Salt, to taste

Fresh cracked black pepper, to taste

1 log goat cheese, 4 ounces (113 g)

Extra-virgin olive oil

1. Remove the lids of the jars so that the jars are ready to fill.

2. In a small bowl, mix together the fresh herbs, salt, and pepper. Set aside.

3. Cut the goat cheese log into fourths, and then cut the fourths into smaller pieces. Alternate layering the goat cheese pieces and herbs in each jar.

4. Slowly pour olive oil into each jar until filled.

5. Fasten the lids on the jars and refrigerate until ready to serve. The olive oil will become firm in the refrigerator, so let the jars sit at room temperature until the olive oil becomes liquid again before serving.

WITCH FINGER PRETZEL RODS

MAKES 12 PRETZEL RODS

1 package green melting wafers or white melting wafers, candy coating, or chocolate chips

Green food coloring (optional)

12 pretzel rods

12 almond slivers

1. Line a baking sheet with parchment paper and set aside.

2. Melt the melting waffers according to the package instructions.

3. If using white melting wafers, add green food coloring to the melted chocolate to get the desired color.

4. Dip two-thirds of a pretzel rod into the melted chocolate. Let the excess chocolate drip off, and then lay the pretzel rod on the prepared baking sheet. Place an almond sliver at the top of the pretzel to look like a fingernail. Repeat with the remaining pretzel rods.

5. Let the chocolate harden before serving.

RAINBOW SPRINKLE PRETZEL RODS

MAKES 12 PRETZEL RODS

1 container rainbow sprinkles

1 package white melting wafers, candy coating, or chocolate chips

12 pretzel rods

1. Line a baking sheet with parchment paper. Add the rainbow sprinkles to a shallow bowl. Set the baking sheet and bowl aside.

2. Melt the melting waffers according to the package instructions.

3. Dip a pretzel rod halfway into the melted chocolate. Let the excess chocolate drip off, and then roll the chocolate-covered part of the pretzel in the bowl of sprinkles. Transfer to the prepared baking sheet. Repeat with the remaining pretzel rods.

4. Let the chocolate harden before serving.

FALL BARK

MAKES 10 TO 12 SERVINGS

1 package white chocolate chips, 12 ounces (340 g) in size

1 cup (100 g) mini pretzels (such as Snyder's of Hanover Itty Bitty Minis)

¼ cup (50 g) candy corn

¼ cup (50 g) Reese's Pieces

1 to 2 tablespoons M&M's Milk Chocolate Minis, using only yellow, orange, and brown ones

1. Line a baking sheet with wax paper and set aside.

2. Melt the white chocolate chips according to the package directions. Pour the melted chocolate onto the prepared baking sheet and spread to about a ¼-inch (6 mm) thickness.

3. Evenly sprinkle the mini pretzels, candy corn, Reese's Pieces, and M&M's Minis on top of the melted chocolate.

4. Let the chocolate harden, and then break it into irregular-shaped pieces.

FALL FOLIAGE PRETZEL RODS

MAKES 12 PRETZEL RODS

1 container fall-leaf or fall-colored sprinkles

1 package chocolate melting wafers, candy coating, or chocolate chips

12 pretzel rods

1. Line a baking sheet with parchment paper. Add the fall leaf sprinkles to a shallow bowl. Set the baking sheet and bowl aside.

2. Melt the melting waffers according to the package instructions.

3. Dip two-thirds of a pretzel rod into the melted chocolate. Let the excess chocolate drip off, and then roll the chocolate-covered part of the pretzel in the bowl of sprinkles. Transfer to the prepared baking sheet. Repeat with the remaining pretzel rods.

4. Let the chocolate harden before serving.

YETI PRETZEL RODS

MAKES 12 PRETZEL RODS

1 bag sweetened shredded coconut

1 package white melting wafers, candy coating, or chocolate chips

12 pretzel rods

24 marshmallow bits (such as Jet-Puffed Mallow Bits)

1 small tube black icing

1. Line a baking sheet with parchment paper. Add the shredded coconut to a shallow bowl. Set the baking sheet and bowl aside.

2. Melt the melting wafers according to the package instructions.

3. Dip two-thirds of a pretzel rod into the melted chocolate. Let the excess chocolate drip off, and then roll the chocolate-covered part of the pretzel in the bowl of coconut. Transfer to the prepared baking sheet. Repeat with the remaining pretzel rods.

4. Adhere two marshmallow bits as ears to the top of each pretzel rod with some melted chocolate.

5. Let the chocolate harden.

6. Add the eyes and snout to each pretzel rod with the black icing and let dry.

POLAR BEAR COOKIES

MAKES 12 COOKIES

12 Double Stuf Oreos

1 package white melting wafers, reserving 12 wafers to decorate the bears

12 M&M's Milk Chocolate Minis, preferably blue in color

24 mini marshmallows

1 small tube black icing

1. Line a baking sheet with parchment paper and set aside.

2. Melt the melting wafers according to the package instructions.

3. Dip an Oreo entirely into the chocolate. Let the excess chocolate drip off, and then place a reserved melting wafer on one side for the bear snout. Transfer to the prepared baking sheet. Repeat with the remaining Oreos and melting wafers.

4. 4. Adhere an M&M Mini to the snout and two marshmallows to the top of each cookie for the ears with melted chocolate.

5. 5. Let the chocolate harden.

6. Add the eyes to each cookie with the black icing and let dry.

CHOCOLATE SYRUP

MAKES ABOUT 1 CUP (300 G)

¼ cup (25 g) cocoa powder

¾ cup (150 g) sugar

½ cup (120 ml) water

⅛ teaspoon vanilla extract

Pinch of salt

1. In a medium saucepan, whisk together the cocoa powder, sugar, and water.

2. Heat the pan over low heat, whisking constantly, until the mixture starts to thicken and simmer.

3. Simmer for 2 to 3 minutes, remove from the heat, and stir in the vanilla and salt.

4. Serve warm, or let cool and refrigerate until ready to use.

5. Refrigerate in an airtight container for up to 1 month. Reheat in a microwave on high for about 15 seconds. If not warm enough, heat in additional 5- to 10-second increments until desired temperature is reached.

RESOURCES

Restaurantware
(restaurantware.com)

Hobby Lobby
(hobbylobby.com)

BambooMN
(bamboomn.com)

Party City
(partycity.com)

LCW Cookie Cutters
(lcwcookiecutters.com)

Sam's Club
(samsclub.com)

Amazon
(amazon.com)

Bio and Chic
(bioandchic.com)

Walmart
(walmart.com)

ClearBags
(clearbags.com)

Aldi
(aldi.com)

World Market
(worldmarket.com)

Whole Foods
(wholefoods.com)

Michaels
(michaels.com)

Trader Joe's
(traderjoes.com)

Williams Sonoma
(williams-sonoma.com)

Sprouts Farmers Market
(sprouts.com)

Target
(target.com)

Crate & Barrel
(crateandbarrel.com)

Costco
(costco.com)

Dollar Tree
(dollartree.com)

INDEX

A

almonds
Classic Jarcuterie, 21
Father's Day Grazing Cups, 59
Game Day Appetizer Cups, 81
Sidecar Charcuterie Cones, 45
Smoked Almond Cheese Truffles, 124
Vegan Grazing Cones, 31
Witch Finger Pretzel Rods, 131
anatomy
add-ins, 13
base, 12
fillers, 13
garnishes, 13
height, 12
skewers, 13
toppers, 13
apples
New Year's Eve Coupe Glasses, 71
Pencil Snack Box, 119
Rainbow Boxes, 109
Saint Patrick's Day Lucky Jars, 53
Sweet & Salty Fall Snack Jars, 103
Tidbit Wine Toppers, 41
apricots
Charcuterie Kabobs, 37
New Year's Eve Coupe Glasses, 71
Personal Charcuterie Boards, 33
Rainbow Boxes, 109
Tidbit Wine Toppers, 41
artichoke hearts: Italian Jarcuterie, 94–95
arugula: Edible Board Crostini, 40

B

Babybel cheese: Fourth of July Fireworks
Cups, 61–62
bacon
Bacon Twists, 127
Bacon-Wrapped Mini Sausages, 128
Candied Bacon Strips, 128
Father's Day Grazing Cups, 59
French Toast Breakfast Cups, 85
Game Day Appetizer Cups, 81
Picnic Sandwich Packs, 121
Bacon-Wrapped Mini Sausages
Game Day Appetizer Cups, 81
recipe, 128
bagel chips: Bagels and Lox Brunch Cups, 87
bags: S'mores Kits, 113
Baked Pita Chips
Greek Loaded Hummus Ramekins, 93
recipe, 127
balsamic glaze
Edible Board Crostini, 39
Italian Jarcuterie, 94–95
Melon Caprese Mini Boats, 35

bananas: Rainbow Boxes, 109
baskets
Farmers Market Gift Basket, 115
Home Run Snack Baskets, 83
beef jerky: Happy Hour Snack Mugs, 79
bell peppers: Crudités Dip Cups, 47
benefits, 9
blackberries
Classic Grazing Cones, 27
Classic Jarcuterie, 21
Farmers Market Gift Basket, 115
Italian Jarcuterie, 94–95
Melon Caprese Mini Boats, 35
Mother's Day Teacups, 57
Rainbow Boxes, 109
Tidbit Wine Toppers, 43
Vegetarian Grazing Cones, 29
black olives: Picnic Sandwich Packs, 121
blueberries
Fourth of July Fireworks Cups, 61–62
Fourth of July Sparkler Cones, 63
Bagels and Lox Brunch Cups, 87
Classic Grazing Cones, 27
Easter Egg Treat Cartons, 55
French Toast Breakfast Cups, 85
Halloween Spooky Snack Cauldrons, 65
Mini Jarcuterie, 23
Mother's Day Teacups, 57
Personal Charcuterie Boards, 33
Picnic Sandwich Packs, 121
Rainbow Boxes, 109
Valentine's Day Chocolate Cups, 51
Vegan Grazing Cones, 31
Vegetarian Grazing Cones, 29
blue cheese
Edible Board Crostini, 40
Game Day Appetizer Cups, 81
Tidbit Wine Toppers, 41
boats: Melon Caprese Mini Boats, 35
bocconcini
Italian Jarcuterie, 94–95
Melon Caprese Mini Boats, 35
boxes
Movie Night Popcorn Boxes, 77
Pencil Snack Box, 119
Picnic Sandwich Packs, 121
Rainbow Boxes, 109
Snackle Box, 117
breads
Baked Pita Chips, 127
Charcuterie Kabobs, 37
Crudités Dip Cups, 47
Cucumber Canapés, 129
Edible Board Crostini, 39–40
Farmers Market Gift Basket, 115
Italian Jarcuterie, 94–95

Mummy Dogs, 129
Picnic Sandwich Packs, 121
breadsticks: Italian Jarcuterie, 94–95
Brie cheese
Charcuterie Kabobs, 37
New Year's Eve Coupe Glasses, 71
Personal Charcuterie Boards, 33
Tidbit Wine Toppers, 41

C

Candied Bacon Strips
Father's Day Grazing Cups, 59
recipe, 128
candy belts
Birthday Party Candy Jarcuterie, 75
Saint Patrick's Day Lucky Jars, 53
candy corn: Fall Bark, 132
candy eyes
Halloween Spooky Snack Cauldrons, 65
Spring Flowerpots, 99
candy sticks
Fourth of July Fireworks Cups, 61–62
Birthday Party Candy Jarcuterie, 75
Saint Patrick's Day Lucky Jars, 53
cantaloupe
French Toast Breakfast Cups, 85
Melon Caprese Mini Boats, 35
Spring Flowerpots, 99
capers: Bagels and Lox Brunch Cups, 87
caramel dip: Sweet & Salty Fall Snack Jars,
103
carrots
Crudités Dip Cups, 47
Easter Egg Treat Cartons, 55
Greek Loaded Hummus Ramekins, 93
Rainbow Boxes, 109
Vegan Grazing Cones, 31
cashews: New Year's Eve Coupe Glasses, 71
Castelvetrano olives
Charcuterie Kabobs, 37
Christmas Charcuterie Cups, 67
Classic Jarcuterie, 21
Italian Jarcuterie, 94–95
Mini Jarcuterie, 23
Sidecar Charcuterie Cones, 45
Vegan Grazing Cones, 31
cauldrons: Halloween Spooky Snack
Cauldrons, 65
celery
Crudités Dip Cups, 47
Game Day Appetizer Cups, 81
Mother's Day Teacups, 57
cheddar cheese
Fourth of July Fireworks Cups, 61–62
Classic Grazing Cones, 27
Classic Jarcuterie, 21

Easter Egg Treat Cartons, 55
Father's Day Grazing Cups, 59
Fiesta Jarcuterie, 91
Halloween Spooky Snack Cauldrons, 65
Happy Hour Snack Mugs, 79
Mini Christmas Tree Boards, 69
Pencil Snack Box, 119
Personal Charcuterie Boards, 33
Picnic Sandwich Packs, 121
Rainbow Boxes, 109
Sidecar Charcuterie Cones, 45
Smoked Almond Cheese Truffles, 124
Spring Flowerpots, 99
Vegetarian Grazing Cones, 29
cheese crackers: Father's Day Grazing
   Cups, 59
cheese knives, 11
cheeses. *See also specific types.*
   getting started, 14
   styling techniques, 16
cheese straws: Mini Christmas Tree Boards,
   69
cheese wire, 11
cherries: Edible Board Crostini, 39
cherry tomatoes
   Fourth of July Fireworks Cups, 61–62
   Bagels and Lox Brunch Cups, 87
   Christmas Charcuterie Cups, 67
   Classic Grazing Cones, 27
   Classic Jarcuterie, 21
   Edible Board Crostini, 39
   Fiesta Jarcuterie, 91
   Italian Jarcuterie, 94–95
   Mini Jarcuterie, 23
   Picnic Sandwich Packs, 121
   Rainbow Boxes, 109
   Vegan Grazing Cones, 31
chicken bites: Game Day Appetizer Cups,
   81
chicken salad: Mother's Day Teacups, 57
chickpeas
   Greek Loaded Hummus Ramekins, 93
   Roasted Chickpeas, 126
chocolates
   Easter Egg Treat Cartons, 55
   Fall Bark, 132
   Fall Foliage Pretzel Rods, 132
   Father's Day Grazing Cups, 59
   Home Run Snack Baskets, 83
   Movie Night Popcorn Boxes, 77
   New Year's Eve Coupe Glasses, 71
   Picnic Sandwich Packs, 121
   Polar Bear Cookies, 133
   Rainbow Sprinkle Pretzel Rods, 131
   S'mores Kits, 113
   Winter Hot Chocolate Cups, 105
   Witch Finger Pretzel Rods, 131
   Yeti Pretzel Rods, 133
chocolate chip cookies
   Pencil Snack Box, 119
   Snackle Box, 117

Chocolate Syrup
   Fourth of July Sparkler Cones, 63
   recipe, 134
   Valentine's Day Chocolate Cups, 51
chorizo
   Personal Charcuterie Boards, 33
   Tidbit Wine Toppers, 43
clothespins
   Sidecar Charcuterie Cones, 45
   Summer Clip-On Snack Cones, 101
coconut
   Asian-Inspired Appetizer Cups, 97
   Yeti Pretzel Rods, 133
Colby Jack cheese
   Charcuterie Kabobs, 37
   Fiesta Jarcuterie, 91
   Happy Hour Snack Mugs, 79
   Spring Flowerpots, 99
   Vegetarian Grazing Cones, 29
condiment cups: Home Run Snack Baskets,
   83
cones
   Fourth of July Sparkler Cones, 63
   Classic Grazing Cones, 27
   introduction to, 25
   Sidecar Charcuterie Cones, 45
   Summer Clip-On Snack Cones, 101
   Vegan Grazing Cones, 31
   Vegetarian Grazing Cones, 29
containers, 10
cookie cutters
   Fourth of July Fireworks Cups, 61–62
   Fourth of July Sparkler Cones, 63
   Asian-Inspired Appetizer Cups, 97
   Christmas Charcuterie Cups, 67
   Easter Egg Treat Cartons, 55
   Edible Board Crostini, 40
   Father's Day Grazing Cups, 59
   Halloween Spooky Snack Cauldrons, 65
   introduction to, 12
   Mini Christmas Tree Boards, 69
   Spring Flowerpots, 99
   Valentine's Day Chocolate Cups, 51
cookies
   Christmas Charcuterie Cups, 67
   Mother's Day Teacups, 57
   Movie Night Popcorn Boxes, 77
   Pencil Snack Box, 119
   Polar Bear Cookies, 133
   Snackle Box, 117
   Sweet & Salty Fall Snack Jars, 103
   Valentine's Day Chocolate Cups, 51
   Winter Hot Chocolate Cups, 105
corn dogs: Home Run Snack Baskets, 83
corn nuts: Snackle Box, 117
Cracker Jack: Home Run Snack Baskets, 83
crackers
   Fourth of July Fireworks Cups, 61–62
   Asian-Inspired Appetizer Cups, 97
   Classic Grazing Cones, 27
   Classic Jarcuterie, 21

Easter Egg Treat Cartons, 55
Mini Jarcuterie, 23
New Year's Eve Coupe Glasses, 71
Pencil Snack Box, 119
Personal Charcuterie Boards, 33
Rainbow Boxes, 109
Sidecar Charcuterie Cones, 45
S'mores Kits, 113
Summer Clip-On Snack Cones, 101
Tidbit Wine Toppers, 43
Vegetarian Grazing Cones, 29
Wonton Crackers, 126
cranberries: Mini Christmas Tree Boards, 69
cream cheese
   Cucumber Canapés, 129
   Everything Bagel Cheese Truffles, 124
   Floral Cheese Truffles, 125
   Lemon Dill Cheese Truffles, 125
   Smoked Almond Cheese Truffles, 124
crescent rolls: Mummy Dogs, 129
crinkle cutters, 12
Cucumber Canapés
   Mother's Day Teacups, 57
   recipe, 129
cucumbers
   Bagels and Lox Brunch Cups, 87
   Classic Grazing Cones, 27
   Classic Jarcuterie, 21
   Crudités Dip Cups, 47
   Cucumber Canapés, 129
   Fiesta Jarcuterie, 91
   Greek Loaded Hummus Ramekins, 93
   Spring Flowerpots, 99
   styling techniques, 17
   Vegan Grazing Cones, 31
   Vegetarian Grazing Cones, 29
cups
   Fourth of July Fireworks Cups, 61–62
   Asian-Inspired Appetizer Cups, 97
   Bagels and Lox Brunch Cups, 87
   Barkuterie Pup Cups, 111
   Christmas Charcuterie Cups, 67
   Crudités Dip Cups, 47
   Father's Day Grazing Cups, 59
   French Toast Breakfast Cups, 85
   Game Day Appetizer Cups, 81
   Mother's Day Teacups, 57
   Valentine's Day Chocolate Cups, 51
   Winter Hot Chocolate Cups, 105
cutting boards, 10

D
decorative picks
   Fourth of July Fireworks Cups, 61–62
   Birthday Party Candy Jarcuterie, 75
   Fiesta Jarcuterie, 91
   Game Day Appetizer Cups, 81
   Halloween Spooky Snack Cauldrons, 65
   introduction to, 10
   Melon Caprese Mini Boats, 35
   New Year's Eve Coupe Glasses, 71

Saint Patrick's Day Lucky Jars, 53
Valentine's Day Chocolate Cups, 51
deli baskets: Home Run Snack Baskets, 83
dill pickles
Charcuterie Kabobs, 37
Classic Grazing Cones, 27
Father's Day Grazing Cups, 59
Picnic Sandwich Packs, 121
Vegetarian Grazing Cones, 29
dog treats: Barkuterie Pup Cups, 111

E
Easter Egg Treat Cartons, 55
edamame: Asian-Inspired Appetizer Cups, 97
egg cartons: Easter Egg Treat Cartons, 55
Everything Bagel Cheese Truffles
Asian-Inspired Appetizer Cups, 97
Bagels and Lox Brunch Cups, 87
Classic Jarcuterie, 21
Father's Day Grazing Cups, 59
Mini Jarcuterie, 23
recipe, 124
Vegetarian Grazing Cones, 29

F
Fall Bark
recipe, 132
Sweet & Salty Fall Snack Jars, 103
Fall Foliage Pretzel Rods
recipe, 132
Sweet & Salty Fall Snack Jars, 103
feta cheese: Greek Loaded Hummus
Ramekins, 93
figs
Edible Board Crostini, 40
New Year's Eve Coupe Glasses, 71
flags
Fiesta Jarcuterie, 91
Game Day Appetizer Cups, 81
Floral Cheese Truffles
Mother's Day Teacups, 57
recipe, 125
flowerpots: Spring Flowerpots, 99
flowers
Floral Cheese Truffles, 125
introduction to, 13
French Toast Breakfast Cups, 85
Fruit-and-nut crisps
Personal Charcuterie Boards, 33
Tidbit Wine Toppers, 41
Vegan Grazing Cones, 31
fruit leather
Rainbow Boxes, 109
Tidbit Wine Toppers, 43

G
garnishes, 13
getting started
cheeses, 14
fruits, 14

olives, 14
packaging, 15
pickles, 14
picks, 15
preparation, 15
salami, 14
shopping, 15
skewers, 15
transportation, 15
vegetables, 14
gingersnap cookies: Sweet & Salty Fall
Snack Jars, 103
glasses
Fourth of July Fireworks Cups, 61–62
Asian-Inspired Appetizer Cups, 97
Bagels and Lox Brunch Cups, 87
Birthday Party Candy Jarcuterie, 75
Christmas Charcuterie Cups, 67
Fiesta Jarcuterie, 91
New Year's Eve Coupe Glasses, 71
Sidecar Charcuterie Cones, 45
Summer Clip-On Snack Cones, 101
Sweet & Salty Fall Snack Jars, 103
Valentine's Day Chocolate Cups, 51
goat cheese
Edible Board Crostini, 39
Farmers Market Gift Basket, 115
Floral Cheese Truffles, 125
Herb-Marinated Goat Cheese Mini Jars,
130
Lemon Dill Cheese Truffles, 125
Goldfish Crackers
Pencil Snack Box, 119
Rainbow Boxes, 109
Summer Clip-On Snack Cones, 101
Gouda cheese
Fourth of July Fireworks Cups, 61–62
Father's Day Grazing Cups, 59
Mini Jarcuterie, 23
Tidbit Wine Toppers, 43
graham crackers
S'mores Kits, 113
Summer Clip-On Snack Cones, 101
grapes
Charcuterie Kabobs, 37
Christmas Charcuterie Cups, 67
Classic Grazing Cones, 27
Classic Jarcuterie, 21
Easter Egg Treat Cartons, 55
Halloween Spooky Snack Cauldrons, 65
Mother's Day Teacups, 57
New Year's Eve Coupe Glasses, 71
Pencil Snack Box, 119
Personal Charcuterie Boards, 33
Picnic Sandwich Packs, 121
Rainbow Boxes, 109
Sidecar Charcuterie Cones, 45
Snackle Box, 117
Spring Flowerpots, 99
Tidbit Wine Toppers, 41
Vegan Grazing Cones, 31

Vegetarian Grazing Cones, 29
grape tomatoes
Fourth of July Fireworks Cups, 61–62
Bagels and Lox Brunch Cups, 87
Christmas Charcuterie Cups, 67
Classic Grazing Cones, 27
Classic Jarcuterie, 21
Crudités Dip Cups, 47
Easter Egg Treat Cartons, 55
Edible Board Crostini, 39
Fiesta Jarcuterie, 91
Greek Loaded Hummus Ramekins, 93
Italian Jarcuterie, 94–95
Mini Christmas Tree Boards, 69
Mini Jarcuterie, 23
Picnic Sandwich Packs, 121
Rainbow Boxes, 109
Vegan Grazing Cones, 31
Vegetarian Grazing Cones, 29
green apples
New Year's Eve Coupe Glasses, 71
Saint Patrick's Day Lucky Jars, 53
Tidbit Wine Toppers, 41
green olives: Greek Loaded Hummus
Ramekins, 93
grissini: Italian Jarcuterie, 94–95
gumdrops
Movie Night Popcorn Boxes, 77
Saint Patrick's Day Lucky Jars, 53
gummy belts
Birthday Party Candy Jarcuterie, 75
Saint Patrick's Day Lucky Jars, 53
gummy candies
Birthday Party Candy Jarcuterie, 75
Movie Night Popcorn Boxes, 77
Rainbow Boxes, 109
Snackle Box, 117
Spring Flowerpots, 99
gummy rings
Snackle Box, 117
Summer Clip-On Snack Cones, 101

H
ham: Picnic Sandwich Packs, 121
Havarti cheese
Fourth of July Fireworks Cups, 61–62
Charcuterie Kabobs, 37
Christmas Charcuterie Cups, 67
Classic Grazing Cones, 27
Classic Jarcuterie, 21
Mini Jarcuterie, 23
Spring Flowerpots, 99
Vegetarian Grazing Cones, 29
Herb-Marinated Goat Cheese Mini Jars
Farmers Market Gift Basket, 115
recipe, 130
honey
Edible Board Crostini, 39
Farmers Market Gift Basket, 115
Floral Cheese Truffles, 125
Tidbit Wine Toppers, 41

honeydew: Melon Caprese Mini Boats, 35
hummus: Greek Loaded Hummus
    Ramekins, 93

I
icing
    Halloween Spooky Snack Cauldrons, 65
    Spring Flowerpots, 99
    Winter Hot Chocolate Cups, 105
ink pens (edible), 12

J
jalapeño poppers: Game Day Appetizer
    Cups, 81
jars
    Birthday Party Candy Jarcuterie, 75
    Classic Jarcuterie, 21
    Farmers Market Gift Basket, 115
    French Toast Breakfast Cups, 85
    Herb-Marinated Goat Cheese Mini Jars,
        130
    Italian Jarcuterie, 94–95
    Mini Jarcuterie, 23
    Saint Patrick's Day Lucky Jars, 53
    Sweet & Salty Fall Snack Jars, 103
    Valentine's Day Chocolate Cups, 51
    Winter Hot Chocolate Cups, 105
jelly beans
    Birthday Party Candy Jarcuterie, 75
    Easter Egg Treat Cartons, 55
    Rainbow Boxes, 109
jerky: Happy Hour Snack Mugs, 79
jicama: Fiesta Jarcuterie, 91
Junior Mints: Winter Hot Chocolate Cups,
    105

K
kabobs: Charcuterie Kabobs, 37
Kalamata olives: Greek Loaded Hummus
    Ramekins, 93
kiwi: Fiesta Jarcuterie, 91
knives, 11
knotted flat skewers, 10
    Bagels and Lox Brunch Cups, 87
    Christmas Charcuterie Cups, 67
    Classic Grazing Cones, 27
    Classic Jarcuterie, 21
    Father's Day Grazing Cups, 59
    Game Day Appetizer Cups, 81
    Happy Hour Snack Mugs, 79
    Italian Jarcuterie, 94–95
    Mini Jarcuterie, 23
    Vegan Grazing Cones, 31
    Vegetarian Grazing Cones, 29

L
Lemon Dill Cheese Truffles
    Bagels and Lox Brunch Cups, 87
    recipe, 125
lemon sours: Rainbow Boxes, 109
lemon zest: Lemon Dill Cheese Truffles, 125

lettuce
    Crudités Dip Cups, 47
    Picnic Sandwich Packs, 121
licorice
    Home Run Snack Baskets, 83
    Movie Night Popcorn Boxes, 77
    Rainbow Boxes, 109
    Saint Patrick's Day Lucky Jars, 53
lollipops
    Birthday Party Candy Jarcuterie, 75
    Rainbow Boxes, 109
loop skewers
    Bagels and Lox Brunch Cups, 87
    Christmas Charcuterie Cups, 67
    Classic Grazing Cones, 27
    Game Day Appetizer Cups, 81
    introduction to, 10
    Vegan Grazing Cones, 31
    Vegetarian Grazing Cones, 29

M
Manchego cheese
    Classic Grazing Cones, 27
    Classic Jarcuterie, 21
    Fiesta Jarcuterie, 91
    New Year's Eve Coupe Glasses, 71
    Tidbit Wine Toppers, 43
mango
    Fiesta Jarcuterie, 91
    Rainbow Boxes, 109
maple syrup: French Toast Breakfast Cups,
    85
marshmallows
    Fourth of July Sparkler Cones, 63
    Easter Egg Treat Cartons, 55
    Polar Bear Cookies, 133
    S'mores Kits, 113
    Saint Patrick's Day Lucky Jars, 53
    Valentine's Day Chocolate Cups, 51
    Winter Hot Chocolate Cups, 105
    Yeti Pretzel Rods, 133
meat sticks
    Happy Hour Snack Mugs, 79
    Pencil Snack Box, 119
    Summer Clip-On Snack Cones, 101
melting wafers
    Fall Foliage Pretzel Rods, 132
    Polar Bear Cookies, 133
    Rainbow Sprinkle Pretzel Rods, 131
    Witch Finger Pretzel Rods, 131
    Yeti Pretzel Rods, 133
mini charcuterie boards
    Mini Christmas Tree Boards, 69
    Personal Charcuterie Boards, 33
M&M's
    Fall Bark, 132
    Movie Night Popcorn Boxes, 77
    Polar Bear Cookies, 133
Monterey Jack cheese: Mini Christmas Tree
    Boards, 69
mozzarella cheese

Edible Board Crostini, 39
Italian Jarcuterie, 94–95
Melon Caprese Mini Boats, 35
Pencil Snack Box, 119
mugs: Happy Hour Snack Mugs, 79
Mummy Dogs
    Halloween Spooky Snack Cauldrons, 65
    recipe, 129

N
Nerds Gummy Clusters: Birthday Party
    Candy Jarcuterie, 75
nonpareils: Winter Hot Chocolate Cups,
    105

O
olives
    Charcuterie Kabobs, 37
    Christmas Charcuterie Cups, 67
    Classic Jarcuterie, 21
    Fiesta Jarcuterie, 91
    getting started, 14
    Greek Loaded Hummus Ramekins, 93
    Italian Jarcuterie, 94–95
    Mini Jarcuterie, 23
    Picnic Sandwich Packs, 121
    Sidecar Charcuterie Cones, 45
    Vegan Grazing Cones, 31
onions
    Bagels and Lox Brunch Cups, 87
    Crudités Dip Cups, 47
    Greek Loaded Hummus Ramekins, 93
oranges: Rainbow Boxes, 109
Oreo Minis
    Movie Night Popcorn Boxes, 77
    Polar Bear Cookies, 133

P
packaging, 17
pairing knives, 11
papaya: Asian-Inspired Appetizer Cups, 97
Parmesan cheese: Italian Jarcuterie, 94–95
pea crisps
    Rainbow Boxes, 109
    Vegetarian Grazing Cones, 29
peanut butter cups
    Father's Day Grazing Cups, 59
    Movie Night Popcorn Boxes, 77
    S'mores Kits, 113
peanuts
    Sweet & Salty Fall Snack Jars, 103
    Fiesta Jarcuterie, 91
    Home Run Snack Baskets, 83
    Snackle Box, 117
Peeps: Easter Egg Treat Cartons, 55
peperoncini: Italian Jarcuterie, 94–95
pepper jack cheese
    Father's Day Grazing Cups, 59
    Fiesta Jarcuterie, 91
    Mini Christmas Tree Boards, 69
pepperoni

Easter Egg Treat Cartons, 55
Rainbow Boxes, 109
styling techniques, 16
peppers
Fourth of July Fireworks Cups, 61–62
Fiesta Jarcuterie, 91
Greek Loaded Hummus Ramekins, 93
Rainbow Boxes, 109
Vegan Grazing Cones, 31
pesto: Edible Board Crostini, 39
pickles
Charcuterie Kabobs, 37
Classic Grazing Cones, 27
Father's Day Grazing Cups, 59
getting started, 14
Picnic Sandwich Packs, 121
Vegetarian Grazing Cones, 29
pineapple
Fiesta Jarcuterie, 91
Rainbow Boxes, 109
pipettes: Italian Jarcuterie, 94–95
pistachios
Christmas Charcuterie Cups, 67
Edible Board Crostini, 39
Rainbow Boxes, 109
pita bread
Baked Pita Chips, 127
Greek Loaded Hummus Ramekins, 93
plantains: Rainbow Boxes, 109
plastic cups
Fourth of July Fireworks Cups, 61–62
Game Day Appetizer Cups, 81
Pocky
Asian-Inspired Appetizer Cups, 97
Birthday Party Candy Jarcuterie, 75
Movie Night Popcorn Boxes, 77
Valentine's Day Chocolate Cups, 51
Winter Hot Chocolate Cups, 105
Polar Bear Cookies
recipe, 133
Winter Hot Chocolate Cups, 105
popcorn: Movie Night Popcorn Boxes, 77
potato chips: Picnic Sandwich Packs, 121
pound cake: Valentine's Day Chocolate
Cups, 51
preparation, 17
pretzel balls: Spring Flowerpots, 99
pretzel braids: Snackle Box, 117
pretzel crisps: Game Day Appetizer Cups, 81
pretzel rods
Christmas Charcuterie Cups, 67
Classic Grazing Cones, 27
Classic Jarcuterie, 21
Fall Foliage Pretzel Rods, 132
Father's Day Grazing Cups, 59
Halloween Spooky Snack Cauldrons, 65
Happy Hour Snack Mugs, 79
Mini Christmas Tree Boards, 69
Mini Jarcuterie, 23
Rainbow Sprinkle Pretzel Rods, 131
Sweet & Salty Fall Snack Jars, 103

Valentine's Day Chocolate Cups, 51
Vegetarian Grazing Cones, 29
Winter Hot Chocolate Cups, 105
Witch Finger Pretzel Rods, 131
Yeti Pretzel Rods, 133
pretzel twists
Birthday Party Candy Jarcuterie, 75
Fall Bark, 132
Halloween Spooky Snack Cauldrons, 65
Snackle Box, 117
pretzel waffles: New Year's Eve Coupe
Glasses, 71
prosciutto
Edible Board Crostini, 39
Melon Caprese Mini Boats, 35
New Year's Eve Coupe Glasses, 71
styling techniques, 16
Tidbit Wine Toppers, 41
provolone cheese
styling techniques, 16
Vegetarian Grazing Cones, 29
pub mix: Happy Hour Snack Mugs, 79

R
radishes
Crudités Dip Cups, 47
Spring Flowerpots, 99
styling techniques, 17
Rainbow Sprinkle Pretzel Rods
Birthday Party Candy Jarcuterie, 75
recipe, 131
ramekins: Greek Loaded Hummus
Ramekins, 93
raspberries
Christmas Charcuterie Cups, 67
Classic Grazing Cones, 27
Classic Jarcuterie, 21
Mini Christmas Tree Boards, 69
Mini Jarcuterie, 23
Mother's Day Teacups, 57
Rainbow Boxes, 109
red bell peppers: Crudités Dip Cups, 47
red onions
Bagels and Lox Brunch Cups, 87
Crudités Dip Cups, 47
Greek Loaded Hummus Ramekins, 93
Reese's Pieces: Fall Bark, 132
Roasted Chickpeas
Greek Loaded Hummus Ramekins, 93
recipe, 126
rock candy
Fourth of July Fireworks Cups, 61–62
Birthday Party Candy Jarcuterie, 75
Saint Patrick's Day Lucky Jars, 53
Rosemary Olive Oil Walnuts
Italian Jarcuterie, 94–95
recipe, 130
round skewers
Fourth of July Fireworks Cups, 61–62
Fourth of July Sparkler Cones, 63
Asian-Inspired Appetizer Cups, 97

Charcuterie Kabobs, 37
Christmas Charcuterie Cups, 67
Father's Day Grazing Cups, 59
French Toast Breakfast Cups, 85
Game Day Appetizer Cups, 81
Halloween Spooky Snack Cauldrons, 65
Home Run Snack Baskets, 83
introduction to, 10
Italian Jarcuterie, 94–95
Movie Night Popcorn Boxes, 77
Picnic Sandwich Packs, 121
Spring Flowerpots, 99
Sweet & Salty Fall Snack Jars, 103
Valentine's Day Chocolate Cups, 51
Vegetarian Grazing Cones, 29
Winter Hot Chocolate Cups, 105

S
salami
Fourth of July Fireworks Cups, 61–62
Charcuterie Kabobs, 37
Christmas Charcuterie Cups, 67
Classic Grazing Cones, 27
Classic Jarcuterie, 21
Edible Board Crostini, 40
Father's Day Grazing Cups, 59
getting started, 14
Italian Jarcuterie, 94–95
Mini Jarcuterie, 23
Personal Charcuterie Boards, 33
Sidecar Charcuterie Cones, 45
styling techniques, 16
Tidbit Wine Toppers, 43
salmon: Bagels and Lox Brunch Cups, 87
sausages
Bacon-Wrapped Mini Sausages, 128
Game Day Appetizer Cups, 81
Mummy Dogs, 129
Snackle Box, 117
scoops, 12
seaweed: Asian-Inspired Appetizer Cups,
97
shopping, 17
shortbread cookies: Mother's Day Teacups,
57
shrimp: Asian-Inspired Appetizer Cups, 97
skewers. See also specific types.
introduction to, 10, 13
threading, 17
tips and tricks, 17
Skittles: Saint Patrick's Day Lucky Jars, 53
Smoked Almond Cheese Truffles
Game Day Appetizer Cups, 81
recipe, 124
snack mix
Sweet & Salty Fall Snack Jars, 103
Happy Hour Snack Mugs, 79
snap peas: Crudités Dip Cups, 47
Sno-Caps candy: Winter Hot Chocolate
Cups, 105
soppressata: Personal Charcuterie Boards, 33

sour apple candy
Rainbow Boxes, 109
Saint Patrick's Day Lucky Jars, 53
Sour Patch Kids
Birthday Party Candy Jarcuterie, 75
Movie Night Popcorn Boxes, 77
Spanish olives: Fiesta Jarcuterie, 91
speck
Edible Board Crostini, 40
Tidbit Wine Toppers, 43
sprinkles
Fall Foliage Pretzel Rods, 132
Rainbow Sprinkle Pretzel Rods, 131
Winter Hot Chocolate Cups, 105
strawberries
Fourth of July Fireworks Cups, 61–62
Fourth of July Sparkler Cones, 63
Charcuterie Kabobs, 37
Christmas Charcuterie Cups, 67
Easter Egg Treat Cartons, 55
Farmers Market Gift Basket, 115
French Toast Breakfast Cups, 85
Mother's Day Teacups, 57
Pencil Snack Box, 119
Rainbow Boxes, 109
Spring Flowerpots, 99
Valentine's Day Chocolate Cups, 51
strawberry fruit leather: Tidbit Wine
Toppers, 43
strawberry wafer cookies: Valentine's Day
Chocolate Cups, 51
straws: Summer Clip-On Snack Cones, 101
styling techniques
cheeses, 16
cucumbers, 17
pepperoni, 16
prosciutto, 16
radishes, 17
salami, 16
sugar cones: Fourth of July Sparkler Cones,
63
sunflower seeds: Home Run Snack Baskets,
83
Swedish Fish
Rainbow Boxes, 109
Snackle Box, 117
sweet peppers
Fourth of July Fireworks Cups, 61–62
Fiesta Jarcuterie, 91
Greek Loaded Hummus Ramekins, 93
Rainbow Boxes, 109
sweet pickles
Charcuterie Kabobs, 37
Classic Grazing Cones, 27
sweet potatoes: Picnic Sandwich Packs, 121
Swiss cheese: Picnic Sandwich Packs, 121

T
tacos: Fiesta Jarcuterie, 91
Tajín: Fiesta Jarcuterie, 91
taquitos: Fiesta Jarcuterie, 91
teacups: Mother's Day Teacups, 57

toasts
French Toast Breakfast Cups, 85
Pencil Snack Box, 119
Tidbit Wine Toppers, 41
tomatoes
Fourth of July Fireworks Cups, 61–62
Bagels and Lox Brunch Cups, 87
Christmas Charcuterie Cups, 67
Classic Grazing Cones, 27
Classic Jarcuterie, 21
Crudités Dip Cups, 47
Easter Egg Treat Cartons, 55
Edible Board Crostini, 39
Fiesta Jarcuterie, 91
Greek Loaded Hummus Ramekins, 93
Italian Jarcuterie, 94–95
Mini Christmas Tree Boards, 69
Mini Jarcuterie, 23
Picnic Sandwich Packs, 121
Rainbow Boxes, 109
Vegan Grazing Cones, 31
Vegetarian Grazing Cones, 29
tools
cheese knives, 11
cheese wire, 11
containers, 10
cookie cutters, 12
crinkle cutters, 12
cutting boards, 10
decorative picks, 10
ink pens (edible), 12
knives, 11
pairing knives, 11
picks, 13
scoops, 12
skewers, 10, 13
toothpicks, 10
wavy cutters, 12
toothpicks
Asian-Inspired Appetizer Cups, 97
Bacon-Wrapped Mini Sausages, 128
Christmas Charcuterie Cups, 67
Classic Jarcuterie, 21
Crudités Dip Cups, 47
Father's Day Grazing Cups, 59
Fiesta Jarcuterie, 91
Fourth of July Fireworks Cups, 61–62
getting started, 15
Home Run Snack Baskets, 83
introduction to, 10
Mini Jarcuterie, 23
Mother's Day Teacups, 57
Mummy Dogs, 129
Pencil Snack Box, 119
Sidecar Charcuterie Cones, 45
Tidbit Wine Toppers, 43
Vegetarian Grazing Cones, 29
tortellini: Italian Jarcuterie, 94–95
tortilla chips: Fiesta Jarcuterie, 91
transportation, 15
truffles
Asian-Inspired Appetizer Cups, 97

Bagels and Lox Brunch Cups, 87
Classic Jarcuterie, 21
Everything Bagel Cheese Truffles, 124
Father's Day Grazing Cups, 59
Floral Cheese Truffles, 125
Game Day Appetizer Cups, 81
Lemon Dill Cheese Truffles, 125
Mini Jarcuterie, 23
Mother's Day Teacups, 57
New Year's Eve Coupe Glasses, 71
Smoked Almond Cheese Truffles, 124
Vegetarian Grazing Cones, 29
turkey
Pencil Snack Box, 119
Picnic Sandwich Packs, 121

U
umbrellas: Summer Clip-On Snack Cones,
101

V
vegan cheese: Vegan Grazing Cones, 31
vegetable dip: Crudités Dip Cups, 47

W
wafer cookies
Christmas Charcuterie Cups, 67
Mother's Day Teacups, 57
Valentine's Day Chocolate Cups, 51
waffle pretzels: New Year's Eve Coupe
Glasses, 71
walnuts
Edible Board Crostini, 40
Italian Jarcuterie, 94–95
Personal Charcuterie Boards, 33
Rosemary Olive Oil Walnuts, 130
Tidbit Wine Toppers, 41
watermelon
Melon Caprese Mini Boats, 35
Spring Flowerpots, 99
wavy cutters, 12
white chocolate
Birthday Party Candy Jarcuterie, 75
Fall Bark, 132
Father's Day Grazing Cups, 59
Movie Night Popcorn Boxes, 77
wine
Sidecar Charcuterie Cones, 45
Tidbit Wine Toppers, 41–43
Witch Finger Pretzel Rods
Halloween Spooky Snack Cauldrons, 65
recipe, 131
Wonton Crackers
Asian-Inspired Appetizer Cups, 97
recipe, 126

Y
Yeti Pretzel Rods
recipe, 133
Winter Hot Chocolate Cups, 105

ACKNOWLEDGMENTS

Writing a book, running a small business, and parenting during a global pandemic are not easy tasks. Thankfully, I have had so much support and encouragement along the way, and I could not have done this alone. These people kept me afloat when I felt like I was sinking. They have shared my excitement, my doubts, my disappointments, and my accomplishments, and they've never wavered through the good and the bad.

First, thank you, God, for putting me on this surprising journey. A couple of years ago, I was at a crossroads. Nothing seemed obvious about what I should do next. I didn't know what direction to take my business, my career, anything. Despite having a successful business, I had experienced so much loss, sadness, and disappointment that I wasn't sure where to go from there. So, I prayed. I didn't know exactly what I was praying for, so I just asked God to show me what's next. He did, and it was more than I could have ever dreamed up on my own.

Mom and Dad, thank you for being the greatest parents anyone could ever have. The foundation of faith, love, support, constant encouragement, and strong work ethic that you gave me is what makes this book and anything I accomplish possible. I am blessed to be loved so well by you. I love you both so much!

Eric, thank you! For over twenty years, you've supported me in whatever dream I decide to chase. You've worked right by my side and constantly lifted me up. You always tell me I can do anything, but I couldn't do anything without you. I love the way you take care of me and everyone we love. You are a gift to this world, and I'm honored to be your wife. I love you so much!

Annabelle and Jack, thank you for putting up with my constant projects and endeavors. Many nights and weekends have been stolen from you because of jobs I've taken on. I hope you know that my favorite and most important job is being your mom. You are my favorite people. I'm very proud of both of you, and I love you more than you can comprehend.

Juju and Lulu, thank you for loving me, supporting me, and making me part of your family all these years and encouraging me. Lulu, thank you for always being my sidekick when I take on more than I can handle and swooping in and helping make everything happen even amid the chaos. You guys bring so much fun to our family and are the memory makers. I love you!

Adria, words are not sufficient to describe your friendship. Being friends with you growing up was fun and wonderful, but being friends with you as an adult is a gift. You take the good and the bad, the ups and downs, and you just stick it out with me time and time again. You always know what to do and what to say. I cannot thank you enough for your support during some of the hardest times in my life. This book took us on journeys we will remember and laugh about for the rest of our lives. Thank you for jumping on board and supporting me.

Sharissa, Kelly, Katherine, Ashley, and Hollee, thank you for showing me what real friendship is. I love you all so much, and I could never properly thank each of you for all you have done for me. No matter if you are just down the street or hundreds of miles away, you are always there for me. You are not just friends; you are family.

Emily, thank you, thank you, thank you! Your wordsmithing skills took my creations to the next level. When I didn't know what to call it, you did! Your quick wit changed my life. Thank you for the term "jarcuterie," truly a gift!

Thank you, Rage, Erin, and the team at the Quarto Group, for finding me and giving me this opportunity. I will be forever grateful for this experience, and I've learned so much.

Finally, thank you to my social-media followers, fellow graze-makers, and customers, many of whom have become friends. This book wouldn't exist without you. You welcome my crazy ideas with open arms. I will always reciprocate the support and can't wait to see what you do with your own jarcuterie. So many of you have already beat me at my own game, and I love it!

ABOUT THE AUTHOR

Suzanne Billings is the owner of Noble Graze, a dedicated charcuterie and grazing-board company. She is the motivator behind the jarcuterie viral trend and has been featured on Today, Popsugar, Bloomberg, and other media outlets, and countless Instagram food influencers have shared her amazing edible creations.

Suzanne was one of the first to bring the grazing trend to the United States in 2016 and has continued to champion the movement. Her background in event management, marketing, and small business ownership has helped make her business a success. She is driven by creativity, integrity, and helping others.

She lives in Fayetteville, Arkansas, with her husband, Eric; two children, Annabelle and Jack; and her beloved best friend and dog, Louie.